SHAREDINTEREST

INVESTING IN A FAIRER WORLD

GW00400975

20TH

ANNIVERSARY

BY SUE OSBORNE

FOREWORD BY HARRIET LAMB CBE

Published 2010 by Shared Interest Society

2 Cathedral Square, Groat Market, Newcastle Upon Tyne NE1 1EH

www.shared-interest.com

ISBN: 978-1-906477-35-6

Copyright: Shared Interest 2010

Designed by: Faragher Jones www.faragherjones.com

Printed by: Short Run Press, Exeter
on 9-Lives FSC-accredited 100% recycled paper

CONTENTS

FOREWORD
By Harriet Lamb CBE

Never has the mission of Shared Interest been more relevant than today, as the organisation celebrates its twentieth anniversary. All around us lies the wreckage of conventional financing which has always failed on social and environmental grounds and has now failed on economic grounds too. The fundamental purpose of finance (that markets serve the economy and the wider economy serves society) was forgotten in the unfettered rush for short-term, personal gain. The resultant recession means tough times for us all. But if it's tough for us, it is desperate for smallholders and workers in developing countries. Having never benefitted from the boom, they're now left paying for the bust. Last year a worker in Kenya told me that he was missing a meal a day in order to make ends meet. For him, tightening his belt was reality – not a metaphor. Every day, we hear from the managers of smallholder organisations that they simply cannot get the finance they need.

For these groups credit has always been the number one constraint. They need more finance, they need to build long-term investments, and they need a flow of working capital – above all else to pay members for their crops immediately after harvest, but also to invest in everything from improving product quality and agronomic practices through to investing in processing. But what was always difficult has now become near impossible. Producers tell us again and again that rural banks in their area have closed down in the wake of the banking crisis.

Which is why Shared Interest is needed now more than ever – to lend to producers and companies dedicated to fairer trade. Shared Interest is rightly proud of its values of love, justice and stewardship – which put me in mind of the words of Reinhold Niebuhr 'Justice is the political economy of love'. As a cooperative supporting cooperatives, Shared Interest is a wonderful way for people to go to the next step in their support for Fairtrade: buying the goods, campaigning for more companies and retailers to stock Fairtrade, but also investing money to provide the vital financial underpinning the fair trade businesses in developing countries and in the UK need. In 2002, I was lucky enough to attend a pivotal AGM of Shared Interest – when it was agreed to lend more to producers of commodities such as tea and coffee as well as handicrafts – and I was struck by members' depth of knowledge and commitment. Shared Interest members are passionately engaged with the complex strategies and the messy detail of how in practice we make trade fair, while also spreading the word among the wider public. Shared Interest members are leading the way in communities from Newcastle to Newquay, creating the beating heart of Fairtrade.

And it is thanks to such informed and dedicated campaigners that in the past 20 years, Fairtrade has gone from a nerdy niche to taking its rightful place in all our shopping baskets, with millions of producers and so many companies helped along that way by Shared Interest's loans. In 2010, sales of Fairtrade certified products should hit £1 billion in the UK alone, with products from Palestinian olive oil to peanuts from Malawi, ice cream to face cream, opening so many more doors for disadvantaged producers worldwide.

Yet there is so very, very far to go if we are indeed to tip the balance of trade in favour of disadvantaged farmers and workers in developing countries. The increased availability of credit will be critical to that next stage, as more producer groups have the opportunities to sell on fair terms and as more dedicated fair trade companies need the financial base to invest and innovate. For it is vital that Shared Interest stays as innovative today at twenty as we were in our heady early days, that we keep challenging ourselves to adapt and change our model and find new ways to working in order to strengthen and broaden the reach of fair trade. Shared Interest can continue to help move the movement forward – investing in new product development and in new producers and new companies, taking the risks to doing business differently.

It is also clear that we must deepen the engagement of the mainstream financial community who pull so many strings in British business. Already we know that as Fairtrade becomes a greater part of British life, it has caught the eye of investors. Today, some major listed companies who face the relentless City pressures of delivering short term profits are beginning to offer Fairtrade products. Could we consider that if a listed company offers Fairtrade, the producer groups supplying them immediately buy shares in that company – so having a stake in their ownership, an ability to represent their views at AGM and to investors? Other companies are still turning the cold shoulder to Fairtrade but could be persuaded to engage if their investors were pressing as hard on the ethical agenda as they are on profits. Shared Interest is the living example that you can invest in social change and still succeed, and as such plays a vital role in winning that wider argument for ethical investment.

At Dukunde Kawa, a coffee cooperative in the hills of Rwanda to whom Shared Interest has lent money to build a washing station, the former President explained how previously: *"People were growing coffee and selling to middle-men who would rob them, giving such bad prices and telling them nothing. Once we realised that, we created an association and started taking our coffee ourselves first to a dry mill in Kigali. Then we realized that by coming together, we could make such a difference and so we thought – hang on. Let's look for buyers on the international market ourselves."*

Today they are proud to sell some coffee on Fairtrade terms but by no means all. So, he continued: *"Pre-financing is still one of our biggest challenges as loans don't come from the banks on time and farmers want to deliver their coffee early, and be paid. Some buyers only pay once their coffee is at the port so farmers have to wait a month for payment but it's much better if we could pay them immediately. We could also help shift micro-loans out to all the farmers."*

As President Obama said at his inauguration, the success of our economy depends on the *"reach of our prosperity, on the ability to extend opportunity to every willing heart"*. Inspired by the beginnings of the quiet revolution that we have all helped create in the first 20 years of Shared Interest's life, we can all embark with confidence on multiplying that change in the next 20 years.

A WORD FROM THE AUTHOR
By Sue Osborne

I first heard of Shared Interest in the Autumn of 2000. I had returned from a year travelling through Africa and Asia on my own and had come back to the UK determined to find a job that would combine my earlier financial services background with the opportunity to make a difference to some of those countries that had inspired me during my time abroad.

I noticed the advert for Business Development Officer at Shared Interest in the Guardian in October 2000 and decided to apply. I was absolutely delighted when I was offered the position and my long standing relationship with Shared Interest started in February 2001. I worked for the organisation through to December 2006, progressing to the role of Business Development Director. Then after a period of maternity leave, I made the decision to leave full-time employment, but have since enjoyed the opportunity to do some work part-time on a consultancy basis for Shared Interest.

My passion for Shared Interest therefore spans almost ten of its twenty-year history and the writing of this book has allowed me to fill in the gaps in my knowledge of this wonderful organisation's history.

I could not have undertaken this piece of work alone and I would like to thank the current Managing Director, Patricia Alexander and Supporter Relations Manager, Paul Sharpe both for initially approaching me with the idea for this book but also for their assistance. I would also like to thank the current staff at Shared Interest for conducting many of the interviews with past and present supporters of the organisation. Their collective input has built up the story that will unfold as you turn the pages of this book.

I would also very much like to thank the previous two Managing Directors of the organisation, Mark Hayes and Stephanie Sturrock for their time and contributions. Access to Mark's detailed personal records helped me enormously when researching the preconception and early years of the organisation.

I hope for all who have had an involvement in the organisation during its twenty-year history, this book feels like a fitting and appropriate record of the journey it has been on. I have done my very best to accurately represent the history of the organisation.

Many that I called upon with questions of times gone past, told me that they thoroughly enjoyed the journey down memory lane. I hope you too in reading this will enjoy the experience and together we can look forward to an exciting future for Shared Interest.

BEGA KWA BEGA

Located in Korogocho, one of the largest slums in Nairobi. Founded in 1991 with the help of the Catholic Church. Women and girls rescued from the streets produce hand-woven baskets, dolls, jewellery and tie-dye clothing

CHAPTER 1
PRECONCEPTION

"Traidcraft and Shared Interest have a common heritage and a shared vision of a world in which disadvantaged producers can access markets and benefit from trade. Our fair trade values and North Eastern locations enable us to work as close partners both within the UK and on the world stage."
Paul Chandler, Chief Executive, Traidcraft

"**Y**ou will need £25m to make it work. You're trying to do the impossible, but good luck!" Donald Clarke, the Finance Director at 3i, Europe's largest venture capital organisation told Mark Hayes, one of his investment managers, when Mark outlined his concept for Shared Interest in the late 1980s. Mark had been exploring the idea of a financial intermediary investing in the Third World during a secondment to Traidcraft, a pioneering alternative trading organisation based in the North East of England.

Yet here we are in 2010 and Shared Interest is a thriving, successful lending cooperative, with a share capital of over £26m, lending money to 101 Fair Trade businesses in 36 countries across the globe.

It is testament to Mark and his colleagues that the organisation that they established has become such a success story which has transformed the lives of millions of people across the globe. It is not just those of us that know the organisation well that can see how successful it is. Others externally have recognised its achievements.

Shared Interest was first recognised publicly when in 1998 it received a Worldaware Business Award, given to a small business which has contributed to viable economic development. The award was presented to Mark Hayes by Princess Anne.

Following on from that, in 2003 Shared Interest was one of five finalists in the Enterprising Solutions Awards supported by the Department of Trade and Industry and won the 'best revenue model' in the Upstart Awards in 2004.

More recently in 2008 Shared Interest was awarded the Queen's Award for Enterprise in the Sustainable Development category, the most prestigious corporate accolade that a UK business can win. The award was presented by Her Majesty's Lord-Lieutenant for the County of Tyne and Wear, Mr Nigel Sherlock OBE, an individual who has been familiar with Shared Interest for its entire 20 years history as a member of the initial steering group considering the proposition of an alternative finance organisation.

In his speech at the presentation of the Queen's Award for Enterprise 2008 Sustainable Development in the Assembly Rooms in Newcastle upon Tyne on Wednesday 2nd July Nigel Sherlock said:

"The Queen's Awards to Industry are designed to recognise and encourage outstanding achievement in Exports or in Technological Innovation or Sustainable Development or all three!

"The Award was instituted by Royal Warrant in 1965, and is made by Her Majesty the Queen on the advice of the Prime Minister, assisted by an advisory committee, which includes representatives of industry and commerce, the Trade Unions and engineering institutions.

"The Award List is always announced on the 21st April each year, which is the actual birthday of Her Majesty the Queen.

"*Many years ago, I had some very small input to the setting up of the Society, though not as Lord-Lieutenant, and therefore it gives me particular pleasure to see how, having overcome some initial obstacles, your Society has flourished and is here today receiving major recognition for your great undertaking.*

"*Shared Interest has demonstrated great leadership in supporting the Fair Trade industry on a worldwide basis. Your Society directly serves to promote the development of producers, providing the opportunity for them to become self sustaining, with far reaching benefits for such bodies and ultimately consumers. As a Society you have demonstrated that there is a strong demand for ethical investments, enhancing regulation and standardisation and ultimately bolstering the market for such investment and trade.*

"*I must repeat, The Queen's Award is not won easily, and is not as the result of efforts by any one individual – it reflects the skills, commitment and overall*

The Queen's Award for Enterprise being presented by Nigel Sherlock OBE

expertise of all of you involved with the Shared Interest Society Limited. The Award is indeed splendid news both for your organisation and for the North East Region. Very many congratulations on your Queen's Award."

Later in 2008, Shared Interest received recognition again when Hugo Villela, Regional Development Executive for Shared Interest in Central America was one of three winners of the forum3 Alternative Rich List. The forum3 Alternative Rich List honours those who work tirelessly for a cause and who enjoy the work they do because it makes a real difference. In 2008 more than 90 individuals were nominated but only three identified as winners, all recognised as individuals who enriched other people's lives through aspiration and leadership.

So we can celebrate the success of the organisation that we know today, but where did it all begin? Developing the concept for Shared Interest is embedded in the history of Traidcraft. Traidcraft was founded in 1979 and itself grew out of Tearcraft (the trading arm of Tearfund, The Evangelical Alliance Relief Fund established in the 1960s). Traidcraft started trading from a small warehouse in the centre of Newcastle with just a handful of staff. Its first catalogue was one colour with hand-drawn artwork just selling crafts. Tea and coffee were introduced in the following year's catalogue. From the beginning Traidcraft relied on sales by voluntary representatives (who later became known as Traidcraft's Fair Traders), who also helped to raise awareness about the need for fair trade. Within just a couple of years, sales had topped £1m and more than 400 voluntary representatives promoted Traidcraft across the UK.

As a consequence of the voluntary representatives' promotion work, Traidcraft began to receive enquiries from a number of supporters who were willing to make 'soft' loans to support and develop Traidcraft's work. As the potential number of loans increased, the team at Traidcraft recognised there was a need to formalise this type of investment. The first thought for Traidcraft was to set up its own bank – 'TraidBank' – but the Bank of England were emphatic in saying no to Traidcraft obtaining banking status – you have to be a bank to start a bank!

So in 1984, Traidcraft became a public limited company and its first share issue – 300,000 non voting shares at £1 each – was substantially oversubscribed. One of the individuals subscribing to the Traidcraft share issue was Mark Hayes, an economics graduate from Cambridge, who was then working as an investment executive with 3i. Mark attended Traidcraft's AGM in July 1984 and fell into conversation with Richard Evans, Marketing Director at Traidcraft and they both discovered a mutual interest: Traidcraft was still pursuing their idea of an 'alternative' investment entity and Mark with a long standing interest in the worker cooperative movement was interested in applying his skill set to making something work on the alternative investment side. His early thinking and that of the Traidcraft Management Team appeared to dovetail and so he followed up his conversation with Richard Evans at the AGM with a letter dated 17th August 1986 to Richard Adams, then Managing Director of Traidcraft. In this letter Mark Hayes outlined his own ideas for a Development Bank. The seed for Shared Interest had been sown.

EXTRACTS FROM MARK'S LETTER

Extending the funding base for Exchange Resource Transfer
I find these two areas the most stimulating, and they set me off on the train of thought that led to TraidBank: Traidcraft's own development bank!

TraidBank would build on the resource transfer concept in a

number of ways, falling within the guidelines you suggest.

The key "transferors" would be depositors and "bondholders" in TraidBank. This would come through their:
a) placing funds on deposit interest free;
b) paying the full cost of money transmission on chequing accounts with no allowance for interest;
c) purchasing irredeemable (though perhaps transferable) "TraidBonds" on which the dividend would be limited and subject to profit in a similar fashion to Traidcraft plc's own dividend policy;

The main returns to the depositor/bondholder would be:
a) ethical banking: remember Barclays and South Africa?;
b) complete security of his funds in current/deposit accounts;
c) TraidBonds would be linked primarily to the financing of capital equipment for 3rd world producers, and could be matched by a lifestyle pledge, i.e. switching expenditure from domestic durable goods to 3rd world capital goods;
d) the knowledge that his capital would be employed in creating jobs both in UK and 3rd world;
e) the knowledge that his interest sacrifice would be used to fund Exchange's technical and other educational work in UK and 3rd world;
f) the knowledge that he would be participating in work to reform North/South relations (similar to a Traidcraft shareholder);
g) a "just" yield on TraidBonds;
h) TraidBank could issue pictorial cheques with a development

message, playing a minor education and marketing role, and reminding the accountholder of the work he's doing every time he makes a payment;

Depositors could include individuals, trusts, charities and development agencies, unions, churches. TraidBank could also provide the liaison and coordinating role with other ATOs who might become depositors and ultimately borrowers.

How would TraidBank employ its funds?
In 3 main ways:
a) working capital for Traidcraft, 3rd world producer groups, and ultimately other ATOs (but see below);
b) equipment finance for 3rd world producer groups;
c) the balance would be deposited on the money markets.

Richard Adams responded to this letter and met with Mark in Cambridge in December 1986. During a chat over tea and scones at Mark's home, Mark agreed to put a proposal to the Traidcraft board in January 1987 with a view to investigating in some detail the options open to Traidcraft. He proposed to negotiate a secondment from 3i in order to do his research.

Fortunately at the time 3i was public spirited enough to allow a venture like this to be pursued. Perhaps it was a tactical move on their part? Allowing Mark time to explore this might get this radical thinking out of his system.

Mark did some initial desk work before starting a six-week secondment to Traidcraft. During his six weeks, Mark spoke to a lot of people, primarily contacts through the venture capital world as well as those given to him by

The original Traidcraft premises in Carliol Square, Newcastle
(Photo courtesy of Traidcraft)

Traidcraft. And at the conclusion of the six weeks, Mark handed over the findings.

Essentially Mark had come up with two recommendations, firstly he suggested a collaboration with the Co-operative Bank managing a pool of ethical deposits and secondly he suggested forming an English support organisation for Ecumenical Development Cooperative Society (at the time known as EDCS and now known as Oikocredit).

EDCS, based in the Netherlands, had been set up some 10 years previously, by the World Council of Churches as a vehicle to allow churches to use some of their cash to help people in the Developing World. It invested in small businesses, often cooperatives that benefited the poor and their communities in the south. Loans were administered through representatives in Developing World countries. Investments were made regardless of race, sex and creed to any viable enterprise that could demonstrate that it would benefit poor people and not harm the local environment.

In response to Mark's feasibility study, Traidcraft set up a steering group to consider what was now termed the 'alternative banking project'. The members of the steering group were Richard Adams, Managing Director Traidcraft plc; Philip Angier, Finance Director Traidcraft plc; Geoff Moore, Principal Lecturer in Strategic Management at Newcastle Business School; Roger Sawtell, Chairman of Traidcraft Exchange; Nigel Sherlock, Director Wise Speke, Stockbrokers; Sue Ward, Financial Journalist and author and Graham Young, Director of Traidcraft Exchange.

The steering group worked in four main areas:

a) the feasibility of establishing a deposit taking vehicle (or 'bank') in conjunction with a High Street bank, which would allow a proportion of depositors funds to be harnessed for social investment, without putting their money at risk;

b) the establishment of a sound theoretical and ethical basis for a critique of the conventional wisdom on investment;

c) the establishment of a legal structure to give effect to the concepts of 'stakeholder' ownership and partnership which emerged from this critique;

d) the devising of a business plan and the securing of the start-up funding [1990 Shared Interest Directors Report and Accounts].

The steering group was established in the autumn of 1987 and Mark Hayes after concluding his secondment at Traidcraft had been sent in September 1987 to Melbourne in Australia to run the 3i office there. He would not return to the UK until February 1989 and in that pre-email era the only option available to Mark was to maintain contact with Traidcraft by fax.

The steering group's mandate was to look critically at Mark's findings. Probing them in detail they found them too conservative and felt he had considered the subject too much from the perspective of a banker. They were not entirely comfortable with the Co-operative Bank managing the deposit pool and the lending decisions therefore staying with the Co-operative Bank. Nonetheless there followed an 18-month period of pursuing the Co-operative Bank.

Geoff Moore in the book 'Good Business? Case studies in corporate social responsibility', in a chapter entitled 'Banking on Concern. Shared Interest Society Ltd.' recalled:

"The first idea was to see if it was possible to establish, in conjunction with a high street bank, an ethical investment vehicle which would fit with the principles being established. The concept was that a clearing bank would receive deposits from investors at concessionary rates of interest. It would invest 25% of this on the money markets for liquidity purposes but would on-lend the majority, again at concessionary rates, to what was called at the time, Project Finance Company plc. This would be an independently capitalised public limited company with both voting share capital owned by a trust and non-voting share capital from the public. Project Finance Company would lend to alternative trading organisations and to Third-World companies.

"The beauty of this concept was that it could involve a variety of investors. Committed ethical investors with money they were able to put at risk might buy the publicly available shares in the company. At the opposite end of the spectrum, those who held money in bank or building society accounts, with little or no risk, might be attracted by the idea of depositing their money somewhere where it would be achieving something positive. The idea also held some attractions to a clearing bank in that there was the possibility of attracting new customers to a differentiated product which would undoubtedly attract good publicity.

"The idea was put to a number of clearing banks. Barclays, the Bank of Scotland and National Westminster all gave it brief consideration but did not feel able to take the idea further. The Co-operative Bank however gave the idea much more detailed consideration and a number of meetings were held with representatives of the Bank. In the end, however it too felt it was unable to support the idea.

"The reason for this was to do with banking principles. Since a deposit with a bank is repayable – there is no risk associated with the investment apart from the complete failure of the bank – banks then feel obliged to retain control of where the money is lent. To guarantee that 75% of a particular deposit pool would be on-lent to another investment company, over whom it had no control, was deemed unacceptable. Even the offer of representatives on the investment panel of Project Finance Company was insufficient to make the Co-operative Bank change its mind."

Meanwhile out in Australia, Mark had decided to resign from 3i and wanted to pursue this project. The secondment had not got this 'alternative investment' model out of his system after all! However although he had made his decision to resign from 3i, Mark recognised there wasn't a clear proposal on the table for him to pursue.

In December 1988 the Co-operative Bank and Traidcraft had reached an impasse, but just two months later Mark Hayes re-entered the frame and put a proposal to the steering group to take the project in a different direction. As a consequence, Mark became a paid member of staff at Traidcraft Exchange and was employed as Project Director.

At this point all of the research and ideas considered were still being looked at within the model of Traidcraft. It was always thought that whatever idea was pursued it would be in the form of a subsidiary to Traidcraft. At its core the steering group wanted the funds raised to finance fair trade.

As Project Director, Mark came up with a business plan. With the prospect of working with the Co-operative Bank ruled out, the company established would need to raise all the funds by itself. So although there was the option in the future for the company to offer loan stock, initially it would need to be entirely equity financed.

The key issue to be resolved was the organisational structure. Two aspects were important: the relationship between the new organisation and Traidcraft and how to establish a constitution in which all the stakeholders felt empowered. Looking at various options regulated under the Companies Act, it was recognised this was going to be difficult as essentially the Companies Act only recognises money not people as the basis of power.

Geoff Moore again recalls in the book 'Good Business? Case studies in corporate social responsibility':

"The resulting organisational structure was, not surprisingly, somewhat complicated. Traidcraft Exchange is the parent, charitable organisation which apart from its own work in development education and overseas business

development, holds the vast majority of the voting shares in Traidcraft plc, the trading company. TraidShare, as it was proposed the new organisation should be called, would have a two tier structure in which the voting shares of the plc would be held not, as in Traidcraft plc's case, by the trustees of Traidcraft Exchange, but by a combination of shareholders in TraidShare. Thus there was provision for investors, Traidcraft plc, TraidShare plc, employees of TraidShare plc, the Ecumenical Development Cooperative Society (EDCS), and trustees of Traidcraft Exchange to have representatives on the Board of TraidShare Stakeholders Ltd. TraidShare would be managed by a Board in the same way as any other company, but would be accountable to the Board of TraidShare Stakeholders Ltd."

In Mark's business plan which he put together towards the end of 1989, he confirmed that he had raised £100,000 towards the launch costs of the new organisation. Traidcraft Exchange had put in £10,000 and £45,000 each had been received from EDCS and the Joseph Rowntree Charitable Trust. In his business plan Mark anticipated raising capital through a share issue of 5 million 'B' non-voting redeemable £1 shares with a minimum subscription of £500,000. The intention was that the prospectus for the share issue would be sent to all of Traidcraft's customers and it was hoped that a large number would subscribe within the mandatory 40 days.

So Mark's proposal was on the table; the funding was in place; but at the very first Board meeting that Mark attended, things started to unravel. Unfortunately Traidcraft was facing heavy losses at the time in principle due to over-trading and excess stock. Richard Adams as Managing Director had left and Paul Johns the new Managing Director came in and questioned Mark's proposal in detail. It ended up with another impasse – the Trustees versus the Board and Mark was stuck in the middle.

In December 1989 matters had reached a head. Mark had expected to raise anything between £1.5m and £5m through the share issue, and had expectations of what he could do with that money, but Traidcraft had their own ideas too. Traidcraft plc had at the time been considering its own financial needs and had concluded that it too needed to raise more equity capital. There was, therefore, an immediate conflict of interest, and Traidcraft plc was not willing to release its own mailing list if this was to be used to raise capital that it would be seeking itself at about the same time.

Ordinarily Traidcraft Exchange could have carried out the capital raising exercise, and distributed the funds raised to the two subsidiary organisations. But as already mentioned, firstly Traidcraft Exchange was not a company, and secondly, the proposed structure for TraidShare, with stakeholder control rather than control by the Trustees of Traidcraft Exchange, would have to be transformed in order to achieve this.

There were three solutions to this problem. The first was that Traidcraft plc simply subsumed the idea of TraidShare within it, and raised funds for EDCS as part of its own capital raising exercises. This though was felt to be a non-starter because it affected the concept of TraidShare and was unlikely to fulfil the need for investment funds by Third World companies.

The second solution was that TraidShare subsumed Traidcraft but this was felt to be too revolutionary an idea! The third option was that TraidShare became something entirely separate from Traidcraft. This at the time also seemed to be a non-starter because without the support of the Traidcraft mailing list, there appeared to be little prospect to achieving the minimum subscription required to establish the organisation.

Undaunted by this state of affairs, Mark began to consider the third solution. Richard Adams was his first port of call and having shared his passion for this idea from its early conception, proved very helpful. Richard had by this time gone on to set up a new ethical venture called New Consumer.

Richard introduced Mark to a number of other individuals who shared a desire to pursue this project. One person to whom Mark was introduced was Chris Ruck, a former Managing Director of the Co-operative Bank.

It was Chris who brought a fresh perspective. Chris Ruck reflected on this time: *"Mark Hayes called me up and I'd just retired as Managing Director of the Co-operative Bank. He told me about his idea for an organisation called Shared Interest. I was instantly excited. My contribution was to guide Mark into registering the organisation as a cooperative rather than a limited company which was Mark's original idea. This meant that we could have re-payable share capital."*

After introducing Mark to the idea that the organisation could be registered under the Industrial and Provident Society Act 1965, Mark then consulted with Keith Brading who had just retired as Chief Registrar. Creating an Industrial and Provident Society solved many of the philosophical issues they had been struggling with earlier on – company law just wasn't compatible with fair trade. Also as an Industrial and Provident Society, the organisation would have a ready-made structure and, arguably more importantly, there would be no need for a prospectus when raising investment.

A new entity was beginning to emerge from the fog and Mark's next task between January and March 1990 was to persuade the Registry to register this new Industrial and Provident Society (IPS). Slowly but surely an alternative entity, created separately to Traidcraft, was becoming more viable.

With the legal structure identified and moves made to register the new entity, next on the agenda was sourcing investment! Back in 1987 Mark had found out about a group of some 200 (mainly Scottish) pioneers, who had gathered under the name of Scottish Churches Action for World Development Investment Association Limited, SIAL. Their Chair was the Reverend Robert Waters. This group had already understood the need for social investment and had put £250,000 behind EDCS despite very limited organisational resources.

Another key player then came into the next stage of the story. Doug Brunson who was General Manager of EDCS at the time, was very interested in Mark's proposal. He had a similar commercial background to Mark and knew the Reverend Robert Waters, Chair of SIAL well. Doug was concerned that the Scottish entity should be protected and supported not least as the Financial Services Act that had recently been passed in the UK made this support association illegal. The Reverend Robert Waters could see that the IPS being created by Mark could be the solution to his own problem. Transferring the EDCS investment into this new IPS would retain the connection with EDCS (something they were no longer able to do in isolation) and from Mark and his colleagues' point of view, it would provide real capital into their new venture. As a consequence the Reverend Robert Waters wrote personally to every member of SIAL explaining Shared Interest and got a positive response from every one. With this support, the Reverend Robert Waters was prepared to agree to invest in Shared Interest.

The Reverend Robert Waters later recalled that without the support and investment of people in churches it wouldn't have happened – *"we made it go!"*

And so, finally after tumultuous beginnings, Shared Interest was established in April 1990 as an Industrial and Provident Society. Its name pays testament to the wide group of people who freely gave their time and skills to the endeavour. It would not be an understatement to say that if it had not been for their efforts, perseverance and on occasion their sheer determination, the lives of millions of people across the globe would not have been transformed.

CANAAN FAIR TRADE

A Jenin-based Palestinian firm committed to practising fair trade along its supply chain. Established in 2004, Canaan markets *"products of Palestine"* which are produced by 41 olive oil-producing cooperatives with 1,100 small farmers

CHAPTER 2
THE EARLY YEARS

"The creativity of people like Mark Hayes has been one of the outstanding features of EDCS. Because people who are committed to justice don't accept the first 'no' when they know the structures are unjust, Shared Interest was created as a phoenix from the ashes." **Doug Brunson, General Manager, EDCS** (Quarterly Return 11, Spring 1994)

EXTRACTS FROM TRAIDCRAFT EXCHANGE TRUSTEES
MEETING (INCLUDING FOUNDER MEMBERS OF
PROVIDENT SOCIETY) 30TH MARCH 1990

Roger Sawtell explained that the first part of the meeting was an informal discussion between the Trustees and a representative of the plc (Paul Johns) to hear the views of the Board about the relationship between the plc and the new Provident Society.

Paul explained that he had spoken to all Trustees about the Board minutes and a document dated 15th February which set out how the Board felt the relationship between the plc and the Provident Society should be. He reiterated the fact that the Board welcomed the project and thought that it was a good initiative and would like to see the Provident Society succeed.

Having heard the views of the plc and having discussed the matter with other founder members, Trustees then discussed how to vote on the name to be adopted.

With regard to the name, the following proposals were made.

- It was proposed that "Fair Trade Investment Society" be the Trustees first choice. Vote: 4 in favour, 1 against with 1 abstention.
- It was proposed that "Fair Exchange Investment Society" be the Trustees second choice. Vote: 5 in favour with 1 abstention.
- Trustees had a further discussion about the name to be adopted bearing in mind that each of them had an individual vote as a founder member in addition to the corporate vote of the Trustees. This was felt necessary as Trustees' opinions had changed in the wider audience discussion.

It was following this discussion that the name Shared Interest was chosen and history subsequently made.

Shared Interest Society Limited was officially incorporated and registered under the Industrial and Provident Societies Act 1965 on 25th April 1990. It described itself at the time as: *"a Christian initiative which grew out of and continues to express the work and objects of Traidcraft Exchange and in which existing investors in the Ecumenical Development Cooperative Society (EDCS) under the auspices of Scottish Churches Action for World Development (SCAWD) became the major initial investors. The Society embodies their joint vision of a new economic order based on love and justice, and carries on their work in a new dimension. The Society was founded on 30th March 1990.*

"The Society's legal purpose is to carry on the business of providing financial services, especially for production and trade, in a manner which reflects the principles of love, justice and stewardship, which are fundamental to the faith of the Christian Church and are accepted by many other people of goodwill and compassion and in order to promote wholesome, dignified and sustainable employment for the benefit of people in need in any part of the world, particularly in poor countries."

In the 1990 Report of the Directors, the Directors noted: *"to this end the Society has committed itself to investing at least 50% of its first £4m of share capital in EDCS, which is incorporated in the Netherlands as a cooperative society with similar purposes. In due course the Society intends to seek other international partners, and to make direct investments in European enterprises which provide access to markets for the benefit of Third World producers."*

The first Directors appointed were the Founder Members, Mark Hayes and Richard Adams and the first Secretary was Mark Hayes. Richard Adams agreed to be Moderator of the first Board meeting held on 30th April 1990 at its first official premises 52 Elswick Road, Newcastle upon Tyne rented from New Consumer, the organisation Richard had established after leaving Traidcraft. The decision to base itself in offices in the centre of Newcastle away from Traidcraft's base in Gateshead was symbolic of the fact that it had finally been established as a separate entity.

At this first Board meeting, the Co-operative Bank, whom Shared Interest were to go on to have a longstanding relationship with, were appointed as bankers to the Society and they offered the Society a loan facility of Dutch Guilders (Dfl) 915,500 (approximately £300,000) for use in hedging the currency risk attached to the purchase of shares in EDCS for the equivalent amount. A year later, in the 1991 Directors Report and Accounts it was noted that: *"a currency loan used to hedge the exchange risk on the EDCS investment was repaid, in view of the stability of exchange rates resulting from sterling's entry into the Exchange Rate Mechanism of the European Monetary System. The directors now consider the exchange risk small enough no longer to warrant the cost of the hedge".* It was acknowledged a year later in the 1992 Directors Report that: *"our expression last year of confidence in the stability of the Exchange Rate Mechanism of the European Monetary System proved premature. Exchange rate risks are hedged through forward sales of currency".* 1992 was of course the year that Britain was forced to withdraw from the Exchange Rate Mechanism on 'Black Wednesday'.

Mark Hayes and Richard Adams had written to EDCS earlier in the month of April 1990 requesting admission to membership on behalf of Shared Interest. At this first board meeting, Mark Hayes produced a letter from Scottish Churches Action for World Development Investment Association Limited, SIAL, in which 166 existing EDCS shareholders requested membership of Shared Interest. They became shareholders of Shared Interest by authorising the transfer of their EDCS share holdings to Shared Interest at the nominal value of Dfl 500 per share. Those applying then agreed to accept share interest at 2% per annum for the first year only and any dividend payable by EDCS on their shares would be paid direct to Shared Interest. Shared Interest Society shares were issued to each applicant with the sterling value of the EDCS shares at the time when sold to Shared Interest Society. This confirmed the beginning of a relationship with EDCS which has spanned almost the entire 20-year history of Shared Interest.

Additional working capital was provided by way of loans from EDCS and the Joseph Rowntree Charitable Trust totalling £90,000 and at its second board meeting Mark Hayes tabled the first set of accounts for Shared Interest which confirmed a share capital amount of £287,000 and a management expense budget of £12,500 for 5 months. The Society was up and running.

Other Directors joined the Society's Board during these early meetings – Peter Gordon (former local director for Barclays Bank plc) and Chris Ruck (who went on to be appointed as Moderator – a post he would continue to hold for eight years). Doug Brunson, General Manager of EDCS also agreed to serve on the Board of Shared Interest in a personal capacity. This gave Shared Interest a privileged insight into the management of its funds by EDCS and also Doug Brunson's experience and skills were invaluable as Shared Interest developed its own investment activity.

With the relationship with EDCS confirmed, Mark Hayes felt strongly that the balance of funds invested in Shared Interest should be used to support other social finance organisations rather than simply deposited with the Co-operative Bank. He recognised that placing liquid funds in this way would limit the cash return but would increase the social return. Other members of the Board though were concerned with the currency risks attached to this approach and suggested investing in development agencies such as Christian Aid, who would give a more secure social return. Although discussed at length ultimately it was recognised that placing funds with other social finance organisations was not an immediate priority but it was one which the Board would return to time and time again over the years.

Sitting alongside the Board, a Council of members was also established to ensure that there was member scrutiny of board decisions. Its early members included Geoff Moore, Roger Sawtell, the Reverend Robert Waters and Graham Young. Geoff, Roger and Graham had all been members of the steering group so were fully supportive of the fledgling Shared Interest. It is interesting to note that the Council was established only a month or two after the Board, to ensure real weight was given to the Society's social objectives as well as to its corporate financial interest. The Council had the ability to scrutinise Board decisions, and it was also acknowledged as part of their role that they should help the Board find new members.

With money in the bank, Board and Council established, it was then time to turn to the logo and brand of the organisation. With ambitious plans to attract investment into Shared Interest it was going to be necessary to have a strong brand by which to identify itself. After consideration was given to a number of designs, agreement was finally settled on a % sign with coins denoted in each of the circles.

Then the focus for both the Board and Council was the launch of the organisation and how to market it to potential investors. Both agreed that a large publicity launch was inappropriate at this stage. Instead the plan was that as soon as the basic literature was available the core networks of Traidcraft, New Consumer and New Internationalist would be used but beyond these it was felt that people would only make investments on the advice of someone they respected. During its history it has always been acknowledged by Shared Interest that the most effective method to drive

The first Shared Interest logo

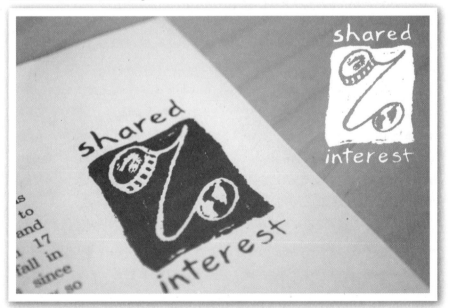

investment is recommendation from an existing member.

Other suggestions that were discussed included using part of the marketing budget to set up Regional Representatives working on a part-time basis to make presentations to the public to encourage investment. Another idea was to find a celebrity who was sympathetic to the issue and use their face in advertising. Once again 20 years on this is still being talked about at Shared Interest as a good idea but trying to identify the right celebrity is still proving difficult.

According to The Independent on 22nd September 1990, Shared Interest was referred to as: *"The new concept in ethical investment"*. The article went on to say: *"We are hoping to reach people who are concerned about development issues, and sensitive to the questions involved. Shared Interest is encouraging investors to consider not only the benefits they receive, but also the help which their money can offer to the people using it to create employment opportunities."* Specific mention was made of the fact that: *"unlike building societies, Shared Interest funds will be placed in the inherently risky area of venture capital"*, however this was backed up by a comparison with banks, by saying: *"The Ecumenical Development Cooperative Society (EDCS)* [via whom Shared Interest made its initial loans] *has maintained its capital when commercial banks have had to write off their Third World loans."*

Similarly, the Guardian on 29th September 1990 called out to: *"Those keen to back ethical and green ventures"* citing Shared Interest as an: *"alternative deposit scheme invested to support and promote Third World employment"*. It went on to describe the organisation as: *"the UK's first 'social investment' society, pioneered by Mark Hayes, with the backing of Traidcraft."*

At the end of its first five months of trading, The Directors of Shared Interest Society produced their first Report and Financial Statements for the period ending 30th September 1990 and confirmed that: *"the profit for the period after taxation was £301. The Directors consider a good start has been made, especially as public promotion began only at the end of the period, and look forward to attracting significant additional capital in the first full year of business to 30 September 1991."*

Chris Ruck, as Moderator of the Board of Directors commented: *"This society is all about people – the people who were given the chance to work for a better life for their families and the communities in the 13 new EDCS investment projects which Shared Interest has helped to make possible in its first five months of existence – and the people who had cared enough about them to invest some £350,000 by the end of that period.*

"The Society is simply a group of people, who have come together to provide other, less fortunate, people with access to much needed business credit. I am sure there are many more people who will want to join us in this work, if we can but tell them about it."

As the Directors recognised that members wished to know as much as possible about the projects Shared Interest supported they included a number of examples of those recently approved by EDCS:

An agricultural cooperative, Bolivia

Asociación Nacional de Productores de Frejol (ASOPROF) is a newly formed national cooperative federation representing 2,000 of the poorest 'campesinos' or small farmers, most of whom live in conditions of extreme hardship. Its focus is on the production and marketing of beans for which there is high demand in neighbouring Brazil, and which grow in the winter when the farmers have almost no income.

As with other agricultural cooperatives its primary function is to finance the planting of the beans and the holding of stocks of the harvest, as well as the related marketing and transport activities. At harvest time prices are lowest, and by storage until prices are normal, the producers can earn income which otherwise accrues to merchants with capital resources. EDCS has invested £94,000 by way of a US$ loan over 3 years repayable out of the export earnings, to assist in this.

A village handicraft centre, Chiang Mai, Thailand
The YMCA of Chiang Mai has been actively involved in development work to relieve poverty for 18 years. It has been mostly involved in community organisation, training and health care, but its Village Handicraft Program, started eight years ago, has become a major source of productive employment as well as vocational training, mainly for women who work from home. 95% of sales are to the local market, although the potential for export through ATOs is being explored.

Sales have grown to the point where new premises are needed for storage, despatch, training and showrooms, and EDCS is providing a loan of £70,000 to finance the construction of a new building on land purchased by the YMCA.

For a handicrafts industry to assist in overcoming poverty requires an effective marketing organisation which has as its aim the benefit of the producers. It is particularly effective when it can reach women in their homes, upon whom the burden of making ends meet tends to fall most heavily.

As noted in the 1990 Report of the Directors the priority for Shared Interest entering its second year of trading was to look at increasing the share capital. Early in 1991 Fraser Dyer joined Shared Interest to run a Representatives Scheme with a view to expanding awareness and ultimately increasing investment in Shared Interest. He had had a similar role at Traidcraft and it was hoped he would be able to develop a similarly successful scheme at Shared Interest. Representatives were used in a variety of ways, doing promotional talks as well as manning stands at exhibitions etc. Each individual interested in becoming a Representative was interviewed by Mark who was able to share with them the detailed work of the Society.

Over a period of time a starter pack was prepared for the Representatives to use. This included things such as: a sample of all promotional material; standard press releases; guidelines for running a meeting of potential members, including games for icebreakers; difficult questions and answers; and a list of other Representatives.

As well as the Representatives Scheme, Shared Interest continued to use promotional inserts in relevant magazine mailings but when it tried to cast the net wider, using for example the ActionAid mailing list it realised that those less attuned to 'justice' issues meant they were less likely to support any kind of social investment. The core mailings such as New Internationalist continued to do well and interestingly the conversion rate from the original New Internationalist mailing continued to rise after 6 months showing a phenomenon that is still true to this day that it can take approximately 18 months from when individuals first hear about Shared Interest to actually investing. As the Moderator of the Board noted: *"You always had to take the time to explain what Shared Interest was to people. No-one just heard the name and instantly knew what we did. But once they heard it they were always generally very interested. It's a great concept."*

The monthly target investment being chased was £80,000 and by November 1991, investment had reached the magical figure of over £1,000,000. Chris Ruck recalled this moment: *"Our first million was a very big affair. It was a day I will always remember."*

Exciting though this early milestone was, internally it was known that

Shared Interest needed a minimum investment of £5m to be able to operate efficiently. Below this figure running costs were very high and so the priority continued to be on expanding the capital base. This raised the question of whether this sum of investment could be achieved by a substantial increase in advertising or whether it required more staff and the recruitment of a promotion specialist. Using financial intermediaries was also considered, but it felt inappropriate to offer commission on any sales.

At all times the risk attached to any investment was made clear. While Shared Interest acknowledged it was similar to a building society, it was not the same as one and therefore it was not seeking to attract people's core savings. What was encouraged as far as possible though were *"interest free"* and *"interest accumulation"* deposits.

By early 1991, the interest rate payable on a Shared Interest account was reduced to 5.25% (from 6.75%). This brought it inline with bank deposits at the time. Within a few months it was agreed to reduce the rate further to 3.5% which was in accordance with the current policy of matching the banks' minimum deposit rate. While Shared Interest had no obligation to advise existing members of a change in rate, they ensured that they did through membership mailing, and each time they received a new enquiry the potential investor was also advised.

The debate over the interest paid was included in QR 5, in autumn 1992. In an article a comparison was made to the interest rate the Halifax Building Society would give you at the time – 1.66% on sums up to £500 (*Halifax Current Interest Rates leaflet 14th August 1992*). The observation was made that as your investment increases so does the attractiveness of the interest rate but it noted that the current Shared Interest rate of 3.5% was not to be sneezed at. *"So if you invest in Shared Interest you can have your cake and eat it. You can help people in the Third World to help themselves and could even be earning a higher rate of interest than you might otherwise receive!"*

As investment increased the Board debated how they would utilise the share capital. As had been noted in the 1990 Report of the Directors, the Society hoped to seek international partners and make direct investments itself. In the 1991 Report of the Directors it commented that: *"loans totalling some £77,000 were made: to Bridgehead, the trading subsidiary of OXFAM Canada, to Traidcraft plc, and to Verdin, a Huddersfield-based importer of Peruvian craft products."* By the publication of this second report, total commitments represented 64% of share capital at the year end. Of course, part of the capital inflow was being used to build up the liquid reserves of the Society and, as had been discussed at a very early board meeting, the policy was to place these liquid funds in a socially responsible manner.

Of course many of these Alternative Trading Organisations (ATOs) were still establishing themselves. One such organisation Shared Interest was in discussion with at this time was Equal Exchange Trading based in Edinburgh. It had a humble start, when in 1979 three voluntary workers returned to Edinburgh after working on aid projects in Africa. They had seen how small-scale farmers were getting into debt due, in part, to the appallingly low prices they received for their products. They realised that aid was not the answer – direct, fairer trading could redress the balance. Along with a sister organisation in London, they started buying instant coffee from Bukoba on Lake Victoria in Tanzania. As a result Campaign Coffee was born and in 1987 the Equal Exchange label was launched.

When a loan was requested by Equal Exchange Trading there was a lengthy debate by the Board, most particularly over the effectiveness of Equal Exchange as a trading organisation as it lacked capital. This was typical of many of the ATOs establishing themselves at the time. Concern was also expressed over how much benefit would be received directly by the producers. With Equal Exchange's primary product being coffee there was also a concern about Shared Interest's exposure to a fluctuation in commodity prices and also Shared Interest's exposure to the failure of a major customer. After these shaky beginnings Equal Exchange Trading has had a longstanding relationship with Shared Interest and grown into a successful company in its own right.

This discussion over whether or not to lend support to Equal Exchange Trading led to considerable debate about other similar ATO investment proposals. It was noted that these types of *"venture capital"* investments were very costly in terms of management time and loss reserves. The Board questioned whether this was the most effective way of using Shared Interest's scarce resources particularly when measured against its prime objective of investing in producers. It was unclear for some whether these small or embryonic businesses were effective as markets for producers, whether they raised unrealistic expectations, and whether in the long run the job could be done more effectively through the expansion of the more established firms through whom Shared Interest already invested.

One loan to a well established organisation was celebrated in the autumn 1992 newsletter to members:

The biggest – direct investment – yet!

Shared Interest has just made its largest direct investment to date of £85,000 through Traidcraft.

The investment was particularly poignant because Traidcraft plc's parent, the charity Traidcraft Exchange, helped fund the setting up of Shared Interest. It was therefore a mark of Shared Interest's development that we are now able to help those who helped us.

The loan will be used to provide advance payments to producers in the Third World, whom Traidcraft purchases its goods from.

These payments are made when Traidcraft orders goods. They help the producers finance their production. For example, an advance to a clothing manufacturer could be used to buy in cloth to make the clothes Traidcraft sells.

These advances can make all the difference between a producer being unable or able to take Traidcraft's order. This is because producers in the Third World, usually cooperatives or community businesses, often don't have access to loans from banks or other financial institutions. So the producers could find themselves in the position of turning down much needed work because they can't afford to produce them.

While the larger organisations played a key role, it was still acknowledged that new businesses were an essential part of the ATO sector, so long as they did indeed offer something different in their marketing approach. It was of course hard to predict at the outset which ones would succeed, and there was certainly a case for Shared Interest acting as a short-term catalyst to help young businesses become established and raise their own independent funding, without necessarily committing themselves to a permanent role, other than to finance producer advances.

While the Board debated the issue of whether to get involved in new businesses back and forth regularly, the Council (the members' 'voice' of the organisation) was much in favour of this type of difficult investment, and felt it was desirable both in terms of accountability and attractiveness to members.

With this debate ongoing and a portfolio of direct investments already initiated alongside the support to EDCS, Shared Interest had itself clearly moved on from its own 'start up' phase and was ready to expand its work.

NAWOU

National Association of Women Organisations based in Kampala, Uganda. NAWOU supports women's rurally-based, subsistence agriculture communities in order to improve the status and living conditions of women in Uganda

CHAPTER 3
NEW PREMISES AND A CHANGING RELATIONSHIP WITH EDCS

"In 1990 we formally appointed Mark as Managing Director and thereafter he was the lynch-pin round which Shared Interest revolved and developed. He used to wear a strange hat, (perhaps he still does?), a kind of trilby thing, and an early Quarterly Return editor, probably Keith Richardson, answered members' queries under the heading 'From Mark's Hat'."
Roger Sawtell, Council member

———•———

S hared Interest entered a second phase of its existence when it moved into new premises at 31 Mosley Street in Newcastle upon Tyne on 22nd January 1993. It was the start of a period when increasingly the organisation was moving on from simply establishing itself and instead was looking to develop a long term plan for its business.

As before, the focus was on getting the share capital in, in order to operate efficiently. Around the time of its move, it had achieved the milestone of £2m share capital, celebrated in Quarterly Return Issue 6:

This figure has been reached on target despite the recession. Indeed during October net inflow of capital (investments minus withdrawals) was almost double the £83,000 targeted figure.

"When we first set up many people thought it was another interesting idealist idea that wouldn't work," said Council member Graham Young. "We were told that money and return was all that mattered to people. Thanks to the membership we have shown that this is not the case. People do put a price on how their money is used."

As Director of Traidcraft Exchange, Graham is doubly happy at the news. Traidcraft funded our initial development costs and it was agreed that £10,000 of these costs, over half, would be repaid when Shared Interest hit the £2m mark.

1,500 people have demonstrated their commitment to the work of Shared Interest by making an investment. But of course it is more than just an investment. Investors are members with power, through the Council and AGM, to influence the Society.

Share capital continued to come in at a consistent rate, interest rates dropped and it was noted in the 1993 Report of the Directors that: "the share interest rates paid during the year were 3.5% from 1st October 1992, 2.50% from 15th December 1992 and 1.50% from 1st February 1993". It also noted that during the course of the year prior that: "1,095 new members joined the society and 37 withdrew, bringing the total at the year end to 2,384 (1992: 1,326)."

In the next year's Report, Chris Ruck in his Moderator's Statement was clearly delighted to confirm that it had been a "landmark year" for the Society in that they had achieved the "critical mass of £5m share capital by 30th September 1994". In fact they had achieved £5.4m by the year end.

While the achievement of share capital was outstanding, this was marginally shadowed by the reality that the new membership levels were not up to target. The focus at the time, which continues today, was to seek to increase the number of members supporting the Society so that there is not an over reliance on the existing members to be responsible for increases in share capital. One of the difficulties the Society had when it came to attracting new members was that it was working with a very limited promotional budget. Increasing this budget was difficult though with so many other demands on the limited finance available to run the Society.

The voluntary Reps Scheme which had limited demands on the promotional budget was proving only partially successful at drawing in investment. In Quarterly Return Issue 6, published in the winter of 1992, it was noted that the scheme had raised around £30,000 since it had been established (by the summer of 1994 this figure had reached £130,000). It was appreciated that there was potential for Shared Interest to make local connections through the Reps, particularly as the Regional meetings they were co-ordinating were very successful at attracting members in the area.

Six months later, Quarterly Return featured a newly-appointed Representative in the West of Scotland, Maureen Burnside and she set out her reasons on why she became involved with Shared Interest with a view to encouraging others to become involved.

What attracted me to Shared Interest?
- It is not a charity but a partnership between people in the first world and the developing world.
- It is aimed at helping people in their efforts for self-reliance rather than imposing our view from the developed world on what is best

for the Third World.

- The projects in which Shared Interest invests must contribute to the social and economic advancement of the larger community, not merely result in the enrichment of a few organisers or investors.
- Preference is given to projects where women are direct participants and beneficiaries. Due care and attention is also given to the ecological impact of projects.
- As it does not seek donations but investments which are repayable to members on demand, it utilises funds which would not otherwise be available to help in developing the Third World.

Despite the efforts of the voluntary Reps, it was recognised that if Shared Interest was serious about achieving a long-term target of £20m or even £100m it would need professional advice on its long-term marketing strategy and how to take Shared Interest out into the wider market.

Of course opportunities were out there to make a significant return on the money invested but the rights and wrongs of such a move were debated in Quarterly Return in the Spring of 1993 in an article called 'The Price of Ethics':

You may be saddened or heartened by the news that Shared Interest was one of a handful of institutions that didn't profit from the fall of sterling.

Many financial institutions are now recording massive profits from speculation against the pound. Shared Interest could have made as much as £350,000 if we too had used your cash for speculation.

Last September we were unable to buy £1.2m worth of dollars to invest in EDCS shares. At the time it would have bought $2.4m. We were unable to buy them because we couldn't at the same time sell them back again at a fixed rate in a year's time: this is known as a hedge.

When we buy foreign currency we always set up a hedge, which means we neither lose nor gain from currency fluctuations. But on Black Wednesday last September rumours were rife about the UK coming out of the ERM. Because of the great uncertainty of the value of the pound, no-one wanted to quote a rate to buy dollars from us again in a year's time.

By the time we could get a hedge the value of the pound had dropped and we could only buy $2.1m with our sterling (at $1.72). So we had lost a potential speculative profit of $300,000 and EDCS's capital is short by that many dollars. By setting up a hedge we have also lost out on a further profit as the pound has dropped still further, as we expected.

To be clear, we have not lost any money. What we have lost is the profits we could have made from speculation which we, like other financial institutions, knew were there for the taking.

"The sort of money that was up for grabs – about £350,000 as it turned out – was a very strong temptation. But our gain would have been someone's loss – in this case mainly the British tax payer" explained Shared Interest's Mark Hayes. *"We took the view that our members do not invest their money to speculate and destabilise their own economy. But it is a classic dilemma – would the end have justified the means?"*

It may also be of interest to know that our bankers, the Co-operative Bank plc, were unique among major financial institutions in taking a similar public stance. Well done, Co-op Bank.

With £5m share capital 'in the bank', Shared Interest was able to start to think about its long-term strategy and this was initially commented on in the Report of the Directors, 1994 in a section called 'Future prospects and plans':

From the outset of the Society's work in 1990 it was recognised that reaching £5million in capital would represent a watershed. At this level the margin we can earn in the long-term on lending this amount through EDCS and a few major ATOs would cover our minimum operating costs.

Now we have reached this point, a decision has to be made whether the Society should continue to develop its own lending capacity, based in particular on its links with the ATOs; or whether the interests of its members and ultimate customers, the producers, would be better served by Shared Interest becoming, in effect 'EDCS UK', leaving all lending decisions to EDCS and concentrating on capital raising within the UK.

It was then debated with the members in Quarterly Return Issue 14 in the winter of 1994/1995 in a piece headed 'Which Road?'

At the next AGM members will have the opportunity to vote on the future of Shared Interest.

At present we are an independent organisation which lends money through partners to poor people's trading organisations in the Third World. Our partners include the Ecumenical Development Cooperative Society (EDCS) in Holland and Alternative Trading Organisations (ATOs) like Traidcraft in Britain. Until this year most of our money has gone through EDCS. This means we already hold 5% of the capital of EDCS and could soon become the largest investor.

The Board have looked at the current situation and have concluded that we must decide where our future lies. Is it as in effect a UK branch of EDCS or as an independent organisation working with EDCS? Either direction poses problems.

EDCS UK

Under this option, we would lend all our capital to EDCS beyond one or two existing loans to major UK ATOs. Our office would reduce to providing membership services only. Our rate of growth would slow down to about 10% per annum in line with the rest of EDCS, both because this was more appropriate for EDCS and because we would not have the current promotion budget.

We would distribute EDCS accounts and newsletters rather than our own, and the role of our democratic structures would change in line with their reduced responsibilities. In all but name, our members would be investing directly in EDCS.

Independence

Under this option, we would maintain our existing investment in EDCS, but would develop additional ways of lending. We would need more lending staff to place the money effectively. We would need to earn more and spend more.

At the AGM, the decision was taken to go down the independence route and as a consequence a new way of supporting EDCS was promoted in the following Quarterly Return:

Bond issue to go ahead

Shared Interest is to offer a new investment option, a guaranteed bond or loan stock, to individuals and organisations. They can invest a minimum of £2,000 for five years in return for a guarantee that their money will be repaid.

The decision was made at the Society's AGM following a vote by members to continue to be an independent organisation.

The Loan Stock issue is necessary for three reasons.

Firstly, it will enable Shared Interest to maintain its investment in our international partners EDCS and hopefully increase it. We are finding it difficult to maintain our current investment level in EDCS because the interest payment EDCS pays us is the same as we pay our investors. This therefore leaves no margin to run the Society on. In the past this was not a problem as the effective interest we received was increased by high inflation and interest rates. But with low inflation and interest rates, it is no longer possible to do this.

Secondly, it will benefit EDCS and producers because we will be able to guarantee our investment in EDCS for five years which makes it possible for EDCS to make long-term investments to producers.

Thirdly, it will enable people to invest more than the current maximum of £20,000 imposed upon us by law.

This decision to move to a slightly more independent relationship from EDCS in early 1995 also reflected an undercurrent of Shared Interest distancing itself that had influenced the relationship during the course of 1994. This distance had been created by what became known as the 'Soros dilemma'. But even before then, there had started to be a divergence of opinion. Shared Interest who acted in many ways like a Support Association of EDCS was part of a European alliance of Support Associations called the Euro SAs. The Euro SAs occasionally fell into conflict with the EDCS Board and this put Shared Interest in a difficult position, particularly as they were one of EDCS's largest investors.

Over and above this occasional conflict with the EDCS Board as a member of the Euro SAs, there was a far more significant debate between Shared Interest and EDCS over a $10m interest free loan and a $150,000 grant offered by the George Soros Foundation. This, when reported in Quarterly Return prompted a very significant response with over 70 letters from investors. In the autumn of 1994, Shared Interest published a Soros Supplement which was mailed out to all members with Quarterly Return. In it they put the EDCS position on the matter, as written by Gert van Maanen, EDCS General Manager and that of Shared Interest, including both a letter from Mark Hayes as Managing Director and the Board statement.

For many members of the EDCS network it was an offer that could not be refused. The funding offered by the George Soros Foundation would enable EDCS to work with the poor in Romania, Bulgaria, Poland etc whose economic welfare had suffered greatly from their society being in transition. EDCS would be able to use the funds offered which would enable them to do this work without diverting funds from the poor in the South. There were to be no strings attached to the offer.

However for others, it was the source of the fund that was the issue. It was known that the Soros Foundation receives its funds mainly from profit that is made on large scale currency speculations. The question therefore for Shared Interest, was whether EDCS could and indeed should accept money from such a source.

It became a debate that EDCS shared with its Board members, staff, outside experts, church organisations and of course its support associations,

Was George Soros someone Shared Interest wanted to be involved with?

George Soros (on the right) as depicted by the Financial Times

among which was Shared Interest. EDCS reaffirmed its mission within these discussions as being two fold:

1. To assist the poor communities of the world in their development as a liberating process directed at economic growth, social justice and self-reliance and
2. To be an example that economic activities can be undertaken on the basis of Christian values without reducing economic viability.

In the 19 years since its establishment, EDCS had given proof that the two missions could be pursued simultaneously and successfully. Now though the Board was faced with a dilemma. Whichever choice it made, one of these two missions would appear to be have been subordinated to the other. An outcome that was bound to make some of its members unhappy.

In the end the debate was taken to the EDCS AGM before a final decision was taken. Both sides had much support and the debate that followed was acknowledged to be one of the best the AGM had heard, with both sides respectful of others' positions. A show of hands at the end of the AGM indicated a divided gathering with no overwhelming majority for either view.

At the Board meeting after the AGM the Board voted eleven in favour, three against and one abstention, to enter into negotiations with the Soros Foundation for the $10m facility.

For Shared Interest once the decision had been communicated they received many letters. The majority in support of the position Shared Interest had taken but amongst the minority, there was a substantial number who criticised Shared Interest for taking a stance, they would not have taken.

In the end, the Board of Shared Interest published the following statement:

"We are sorry that the EDCS Board has decided to accept the offer of a $10m loan from the profits of currency speculation, subject to certain conditions. We are clarifying these conditions and their acceptance or otherwise by the Soros Foundation, with the EDCS Board and will advise members of the outcome.

"In the meantime, we wish to affirm the positive value of our present relationship with EDCS and its importance to us as a means of enabling funds of our members to be used by people in the Third World in their struggle for self sufficiency.

"Since we cannot be held responsible for the EDCS Board decision, and since the return on our investment in EDCS is fixed and Shared Interest will not profit from the Soros loan, we do not consider that Shared Interest has been compromised by a continuing relationship with EDCS. We do not, therefore, intend to withdraw or reduce our investment in EDCS – indeed it would be quite improper for us to do so.

"On the other hand, we believe that EDCS policy on the Soros question and other, less controversial, matters does not fully reflect the views and interests of our members. As relative newcomers to the EDCS family we cannot expect major changes simply for our benefit. It is therefore now clear to us that our continuing relationship with EDCS needs to recognise the distinctive identity of Shared Interest and to enable us to develop in our own way, but in collaboration with our friends at EDCS. We will continue to consult our members, in particular through the members' Council."

This statement marked the start of the inevitable separation from EDCS and it seemed unlikely that Shared Interest would ever become 'EDCS UK'. Indeed the more arms length approach of working alongside EDCS rather than through it appeared to now be the way forward.

The developing relationship with EDCS and its inevitable impact on the future direction of Shared Interest fed into a wider debate Shared Interest was having with its members on its own future.

Back at a board meeting in May 1993, the Board had first debated a vision for the future, looking ahead to 2001. One or two directors felt the debate was premature, feeling that they could not commit themselves to major new ventures until the £5m share capital figure had been reached. Others saw the potential of Shared Interest to be a platform to influence the wider social investment market. Perhaps the focus should be on something other than Third World financial intermediaries? Others felt that if they reached the £5m with growth continuing at a rapid rate, the market image of Shared Interest should remain clear and the development of a Third World network of financial intermediaries was natural. Growth should be step by step and not diversified into other aspects of social investment. Mark favoured development of a Third World network through financial intermediaries serviced from the UK, as opposed to extension into personal financial services, a focus on another industry segment, or establishing local overseas offices. He felt they should not be afraid of setting an ambitious capital target: £50m by 2001 was not unrealistic in his opinion, if they had the right product.

Of course, the nature of the organisation being as it is the debate was taken out to the wider membership during the course of three editions of Quarterly Return between the summer and winter of 1993. In the first article in Quarterly Return, Shared Interest offered four main views on the way forward, under the title 'What should Shared Interest be like in the year 2001?':

1. Steady as she goes
Shared Interest should continue on a growth path much as it has

been doing with any changes being only those commensurate with a larger organisation.

2. More control to members
The Society could break up into a federation of regionally based groups of about 500 members. Each area would be autonomous, elect its own Board and make its own investment decisions. However they would still be serviced by a central administration function.

3. Diversification into personal finance
The Society could offer a range of social investment and finance services to members. For example, we could set up a Social Investment Trust or offer banking facilities.

4. Diversification in investment options
At present members' investments go into one fund, but they could go into targeted funds aimed, for example, at a specific project or projects in a given country. There could also be a range of risk options – members could invest in higher risk projects which offered either a higher social return, financial return or both.

While it was clearly put to members that the options were not mutually exclusive they were invited to detail their preference or indeed offer other suggestions.

The response from members to the four options was then tabled in the next Quarterly Return published in autumn 1993.

By far the most popular choice with the members was for Shared Interest to continue very much as it is. Option four was the second most popular option with few people disagreeing with it. Though a few people did think it might divert money into *"popular"* causes. The second and third options were most strongly opposed with concerns over Shared Interest becoming a large unaccountable bureaucracy and as far as offering personal financial services were concerned, there was a concern that Shared Interest might be replicating services already available through organisations such as the Co-operative Bank. Some members offered other suggestions, one proposing a long-term vision for Shared Interest that it should be: *"An organisation the size and stature of Oxfam, but devoted to investment."*

In the summer of 1995 Shared Interest confirmed it was: *"set on a pioneering course as we find new ways of lending to Third World producer organisations."* In its Quarterly Return article, 'Breaking New Ground' it confirmed its lending strategy was emerging with two key elements:

How the members voted

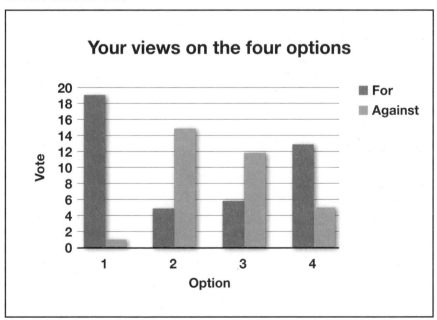

- The provision of export finance to Third World producer organisations.
- Investment in Third World and international credit organisations (such as EDCS) which make loans to producers with domestic markets.

The scene was set and Shared Interest in its newly independent state was ready to develop and expand its work. But first it needed to recruit more staff to take the organisation forward. In the spring of 1995, Quarterly Return confirmed:

Shared Interest expands!

Over the next few months, Shared Interest plans to employ an extra three staff, a Promotion Officer, Administrative Assistant and Lending Officer.

The Society currently employs two full time and one part time staff members. Shared Interest's recent rapid growth has stretched the current staff to their limit. The Board has agreed that we need more staff to cover further growth.

The new Promotion Officer is Allison Barrett. She will have two key roles. Firstly the in-house production of all Shared Interest's publicity materials. She will take over the production of Quarterly Return, devise press adverts and be able to meet the demands for more varied and flexible promotional materials. She will also be able to provide greater support to the Voluntary Representatives Scheme and thus help the

Society capitalise on the voluntary support of our membership.

The Administrative Assistant, Lynn Fairhurst, will help Dot Toase, our Office Manager, deal with our growing membership and the increased demand for information about Shared Interest.

The final new member of the team is to be a Lending Officer. We are looking for someone with experience of trade finance and the ability to assess the credit status of producers. If any members know of someone who may be interested, please ask them to get in touch.

Allison Barrett recalls these times: *"It was exciting to be part of the pioneer years of Shared Interest. When I joined there was a staff of just 2.5 including the founder Mark Hayes and things moved at great speed as Mark developed the systems for providing fair trade finance. My first job at Shared Interest was to explain this shifting system in every forum – to the public through promotional materials and by developing a group of voluntary Representatives to spread the word, and to the members through the newsletter and regional meetings. I have many fond memories of the members and the voluntary representatives at that time as together we found ways to promote the work of Shared Interest, and there was a real sense of camaraderie and dedication to fair trade and the producers."*

With an increasing staff team and growing independence from EDCS, Shared Interest was increasingly looking to fulfil its potential to grow its direct investment and carve its own path in the social investment market.

PROAGROIN

Fundación Proagroin provides essential services
– such as technical assistance, credit, training
and export opportunities– to small- and
medium-scale pineapple farmers in northern
Costa Rica

CHAPTER 4
MOVING FORWARD
WITH INDEPENDENCE

"As the meeting began, I reflected that there can't be many business meetings which begin with a prayer, and where people feel comfortable enough to bring their children with them.

"For me these thoughts reinforced something which I feel is very important about Shared Interest and that is the sense of 'family'.

"In a world where there is great economic injustice, perhaps it can seem that whatever we do is a drop in the ocean. However, at this year's meeting, I had an overwhelming sense that investing in Shared Interest is one of the most positive ways to redress the balance."
Ann Brown, member describing how she felt after attending the third Shared Interest AGM in Newcastle. (Quarterly Return, Issue 11, Spring 1994)

F our years after the inception of the organisation, Shared Interest had quite a different feel. Now fully established it was looking forward and considering how to engage with a wider audience. At the beginning of 1994 money was spent on new promotional literature after it was recognised that the previous literature was more than two years old and whilst it had been appropriate in the early days, the organisation had now moved on and

Examples of early Shared Interest literature

needed a fresh set of literature. There was some debate over whether the Christian basis of the organisation should feature more prominently in the initial advert and also over whether to use 100% recycled paper.

Interestingly at this time, Shared Interest started to promote investment in Shared Interest by using the strapline 'Help create a real job'. The full advert within Quarterly Return that ran from late in 1992 was as follows:

HELP CREATE A REAL JOB!

Jobs that pay a living wage are in scarce supply in developing countries.

Through Shared Interest you can help create jobs that will give a secure future not just to a worker but also to his or her family.

In under two years with a fund that has grown to £1.8m
Shared Interest has created or secured over 450 jobs.
If you want to add to this number, while expecting to obtain
repayment of your money, with interest, when you need it –
Invest in Shared Interest

Over the years this banner message within Quarterly Return changed. From 1995 it read:

**MAKE YOUR MONEY
WORK FOR JUSTICE!**
Poor people in the South don't lack the skills or will to work.
What they lack is the cash to create jobs that will earn them
a decent wage and allow them to live with dignity.
Through Shared Interest, you can provide this cash and get
it back when you need it, with interest. You can join a
partnership of equals to redress one of the greatest injustices
of all – poverty.
Invest in Shared Interest, Invest in People

and just a few editions later it changed again but this time the message lasted for more than five years (albeit the minimum amount allowable changed to £100 in 1996 after a vote at the AGM that year on a motion proposed by the Council):

Invest in change

Opening an account with Shared Interest is about being a part of a movement for change, a change to the present unjust system of world trade and finance, and a change in the lives of those who are not being given a fair chance. Whether you invest the maximum £20,000 or the minimum £250 you take a stand against injustice and help to change the world.

Act now, open an account!

The minimum shareholding of £100 was proposed by the Council as they argued that it would enable more people, especially young people to have an initial stake in Shared Interest, which could grow over the years. Some Board members at the time had their reservations as it was acknowledged that members investing £100 would cost Shared Interest money, as the money earned on £100 would barely cover the cost of the quarterly mail outs let alone the running costs of Shared Interest such as staff time. With the revised minimum shareholding approved, Moira Gilpin was the first person to take advantage of the new £100 minimum to open an account. She said at the time: *"I would have invested in Shared Interest at the old £250 minimum but not with such alacrity. I intend to add regularly to the £100 but not yet at specified intervals."*

By the middle of 1996, the promotion activity had done what it needed to do and share capital and loan stock had reached £10m. The decision was taken by the Board to make some publicity out of this immediately rather than waiting for Quarterly Return, through interviews with selected journalists.

It was of course, later celebrated in Quarterly Return Issue 21, Autumn

1996 when Mark Hayes said: *"We had hoped we could be there by our financial year end, at the end of September, but the figure was reached on 8th July. New members are coming in at the expected rate, but the level of reinvestment by existing members has exceeded our expectations. Hopefully this is a sign of increasing confidence in Shared Interest and growing commitment to what we do."*

In the article Mark went on to report that rapid growth brought with it its own problems however, and this was compounded by the decision to become independent from EDCS and by the need to work out the *"nitty gritty of a new lending system"*. He noted that the staff, especially in the Finance section were being stretched beyond the limit, and were under-resourced to keep up with the pace of change.

"Our costs compare very well with ordinary financial organisations but we need now to catch up with ourselves" said Mark Hayes. *"Already in the past 18 months we have had to double our staff. Now, in the coming year we intend to increase our staff from six to nine. As well as an Operations Director who we hope to appoint soon, and who will relieve me of some of the management and lending responsibility, we have created posts for a Producer Liaison Officer and another Finance Assistant.*

"The role of the Producer Liaison Officer will be to enable us to have a more direct link with producer groups and help to build their confidence in us.

"We also wish to appoint a part-time Secretary to the Board (up to 20 days per annum). The post would suit a retired lawyer or company secretary."

The finance post was made available after the resignation of Dorothy Toase, known to many simply as Dot. She had been the first official member of staff after Mark Hayes to be appointed and was acknowledged by Mark as a significant person in those early days. Indeed at the time of her resignation in the summer of 1996, the Board placed on record their recognition of her value to the Society since its inception and did everything they could to persuade her to stay on as Company Secretary.

Colin Crawford was appointed as Operations Director in December 1996. Colin at the time had recently retired from international banking and was working for the Glasgow Chamber of Commerce when a friend sent him the job specification for the role of Operations Director at Shared Interest.

Colin said: *"The role suited me down to the ground. I decided to apply and came to Newcastle for an intense day of interviews with Board and staff members, of whom there were only four at the time plus a few temps. I was very impressed after speaking to Mark about the organisation and seeing first hand his and others motivation for working for Shared Interest. I discovered just how unique the organisation was. It was setting out to change the face of fair trade – offering a type of finance that had never been available before. I was offered the job, took it and moved to Newcastle."*

It was a position he would hold for eight years before retiring in 2004. At the time of his retirement he reflected on his time at Shared Interest: *"We have all heard the sayings that every journey, not matter how long, begins with a single step and that it is better to travel than to arrive. Eight years ago when I joined Shared Interest I took my first step on a fair trade journey and I am still travelling. I long ago realised that it is not the places you visit that are most important it's the people you meet and I'm not going to mention one or two because that would be unfair. But perhaps a couple of my most poignant memories were being asked to say the Selkirk Grace before enjoying a meal under a Kenyan evening sky covered in stars and receiving a gift of a few grains of sugar when I visited the home of a wonderful woman in the slums of Bombay. She had nothing else to give me but insisted that I could not leave her home without receiving hospitality."*

(Quarterly Return, Issue 53, Autumn 2004)

Back in 1996, the expanding staff team was necessary as Mark had said to take account of the new increase in direct lending. The proposals that were coming in were now wide and varied, for example:

A facility was approved for Candela Peru, a non-profit alternative trading organisation. Candela Peru was founded in 1989 and was set up to work with brazil nut gatherers and their families who live along the Madre de Dios River in the Peruvian rainforest. The organisation offers training to the nut gatherers on administration, sustainable resource management, and export procedures.

Candela's brazil nuts are harvested from trees that grow naturally in the rainforest and reach heights of over 150 feet. The nut pods fall from the trees, are gathered, and then the pods are cracked open with machetes to extract the nuts, which are used for food or oil. The nut gatherers' livelihood depends on the sound management of forest resources, and they work closely with the staff of Candela to improve the quality of their organic product.

The early relationship that Shared Interest developed with Candela Peru, proved to be invaluable some five years later, as explained by Gaston Vizcarra, Candela Peru: "with the collapse in the brazil nut market in Peru in 2002 we had to use our ingenuity to find new products to sell using the nuts gathered in the forest. We developed a natural oil and with much hard work secured a large order from a commercial buyer. However we would not have been able to produce the order without the finance from Shared Interest." (Annual Report, for year end September 2002)

Another organisation Shared Interest built an early relationship with was Community Aid Abroad Trading (who later went on to become known as Oxfam Australia Trading). This organisation which had started out as the Food for Peace Campaign in the 1950s had grown to become Community Aid Abroad and in 1965 established Trade Action to provide trade opportunities between Australia and developing countries by selling handicrafts. From 1965 to 1976 Trade Action ran profitably and subsidised the organisation's operating costs, but its performance declined and it was sold in 1979. Local groups continued to trade with project partners, and in 1986 these efforts were combined to form CAA Trading, which by 2005 incorporated 17 shops across Australia, and mail order and wholesale operations in Adelaide. These ventures went on to form the basis of the Oxfam Shop which has been expanding in recent years, selling fair trade goods. This was another customer who would go on to have a long standing relationship with Shared Interest. As Paul Deighton, Oxfam Australia Trading commented some years later: *"During 2003, just over one million US dollars was paid to artisans via Shared Interest on our behalf. This is a model for community living on a global scale. Getting the message out that together we can make a difference will inspire others."*

In the US at the time fair trade was also growing and organisations such as SERRV were keen to build a relationship with Shared Interest. As an organisation, it also had very humble beginnings – a small group of church relief workers helping refugees in Europe recover economically and socially and rebuild after World War II. (The name SERRV was originally an acronym for Sales Exchange for Refugee Rehabilitation and Vocation). Now it works with producers worldwide and is one of the largest and well thought of fair trade organisations. Bob Chase of SERRV recalls: *"From our beginnings we were part of the Church of the Brethren, they financed our entire inventory. However they recognised that we needed to become independent and make the transition of financing our own inventory. Even though we had been trading for many years commercial banks still viewed us as a start up business. Mark Hayes and Colin Crawford worked closely with us and provided us with the facility we still operate today. I can say unequivocally that we would not be where we are today without the support of Shared Interest."*

With the number of organisations Shared Interest was starting to work with increasing, the annual board strategy meeting, held in May each year, took on a slightly different meaning. In 1996, the commitment to financing fair trade was reaffirmed with the emphasis that fair trade was not synonymous with existing ATOs. While the ATOs would have enough demand to absorb Shared Interest's funds over the next three years, their longer term future was not clear and Shared Interest should have the next stage identified long before then. It was agreed that it needed to diversify its risk.

The real aim it was agreed should be on producers and early progress should be made in establishing the direct credit relationships which were the ultimate aim of Shared Interest's involvement with ATOs. It was acknowledged though that realistically the support from Shared Interest would have to concentrate on those producers that were generating export earnings in order to be able to repay hard currency loans.

In order to increase its potential to loan to the fair trade world, it was agreed that an approach should be made to the International Fair Trade Association (IFAT) to give consideration to a strategic engagement. This alone should not be the only option considered to take Shared Interest beyond the three year plan period.

At this point in time the Directors therefore approved a strategy which included a doubling of assets over three years to £20m, a 4% margin between the share interest rate given to members and wholesale market interest rates and a 1% trading profit margin on the main business.

On the question of interest rate, it was resolved to adopt a policy of maintaining over time the present 4% differential from wholesale money market deposit rates, noting that this placed Shared Interest's rate about 1.5% below the market rate. It was agreed that Shared Interest would not seek to move nearer to the market rate for the time being. The exact timing of changes in Shared Interest's rate would depend on the reaction of retail market "competitors" such as the building societies to changes in the wholesale rate. The question of the relationship between Shared Interest's rate and the market's it was agreed could usefully be debated in Quarterly Return.

According to correspondence at the time, member reaction to this was positive. The majority welcomed the acknowledgement that we were not in a position to be as competitive as building societies, re-iterating that this was all part of 'sharing the interest' to have the impact we desired. Furthermore, suggestions were made that interest should not be paid on any account between £100 and £250 and that members should have the right to waive interest.

As part of its over arching strategy discussion, it was also agreed as a general principle that Shared Interest should continue to be involved in microcredit which at the time it did through its relationship with EDCS. Although there was some frustration expressed by Directors that the best they could do at the present time was to provide low interest low risk loans to EDCS and other similar intermediaries that may emerge.

Interestingly around this time, a letter came in from a member struggling to understand what Shared Interest was trying to do and the following points were published in Quarterly Return Issue 22, in the winter of 1996/1997 to clarify its current strategy:

The whole business of lending money to people in the Third World is complex and costly. Many of our members imagine that a producer group or group of producers simply ask for a loan for a particular project and we send it. A charity could do this because it would not have to worry about repayment, but we have to ensure that our members can get their money back!

As we deal in small loans which cannot support such costs, we have always had to use some sort of intermediary. Initially this was EDCS but from the outset we knew this was a short-term measure, as the interest they could pay us in the long run barely covers the interest we pay to our members, let alone the running costs of Shared Interest.

Lending to Third World producers is expensive, and we do need to be repaid in hard currency if we are to be a viable business. This is what ties us to enterprises involved in export; but this is specifically to fair trade export as the reason for our involvement is to address those very issues of debt and world trade which cause so much poverty.

Our business is to lend money to those in the Third World who are unable to obtain loans from banks and whose enterprises, often co-operatives are run for the benefit of disadvantaged producers.

The fair trade network is the obvious route for us to reach producers as they have the necessary relationships with them, but there is more to fair trade than the handicrafts market. The fair trade buyers are now concentrating more on foodstuffs, fairly traded tea and coffee, honey, dried fruit and nuts etc. This is an exciting market as even the large supermarkets here are beginning to respond to consumer pressure to introduce fairly traded foods.

A year later, in 1997 at the strategy review there was agreement that the Society's strategic direction was satisfactory and pleasure that the financial projections prepared for the strategy review in 1996 had proved accurate except that the trade loan portfolio was growing slower than predicted.

They returned again to the subject of microcredit acknowledging that there were disagreements, now and then, with EDCS but the general policy of cooperating with them and avoiding outright confrontation was endorsed. EDCS's lending policies and practices did however remain a cause of concern, as they were not in line with Shared Interest's mission.

Around this time, after a number of earlier conversations, Christian Aid had expressed an interest in lending their name to Loan Stock 2002 as they saw it as a risk-free way of releasing funds to microcredit and to EDCS. This idea was thoroughly discussed by the Board of Shared Interest as it added a layer of complication to their relationship with EDCS. It was noted that it might be possible for some of Christian Aid's present involvement in microcredit to be funded by loans to producers from EDCS linked to lending from the Society to EDCS. After much debate, the proposal for Christian Aid to be involved in Loan Stock 2002 was endorsed by the Society's Board.

While the Christian Aid involvement might mean in effect earmarking some of the proceeds from Loan Stock 2002, there was a general feeling that the proceeds should be distributed more widely than just to EDCS. Mark's proposal was that £400,000 of the cash should be guaranteed to EDCS and that there should be a tender process for the remainder. This led to a long discussion about the precise way to structure such a tender with concern not to damage relationships with EDCS being balanced by a desire to expand the Society's involvement with other organisations such as the Mennonite Ecumenical Development Association (MEDA). There were also worries that the preparation of the tender process might be too demanding on the staff's time. Further discussion centred on the size of the Loan Stock 2002 issue and the minimum subscription. A minimum of £1,000 was rejected as too low. Finally Mark was asked to bring firm proposals for the issue to the Board meeting in July 1997 for approval having weighed all the concerns.

When the Board returned at a later meeting to the Loan Stock discussion, it was agreed that the next Loan Stock would be advertised in the October 1998 issue of Quarterly Return. It was confirmed that the obligation to EDCS was to maintain an investment of £2m. This level would be maintained if the Loan Stock was offered successfully in October 1998 and issued in May 1999. It was noted that it was difficult to promote the Loan Stock any earlier as there were constraints of staff time required to support the implementation of a new issue even if the administration were outsourced. The involvement of Christian Aid, even though much welcomed by EDCS, did not now seem likely to happen in time for the next Loan Stock or at all. There was a discussion of how to influence Christian Aid so that they came to an early, favourable decision.

It was finally agreed to launch a Loan Stock in October 1998, trying to involve Christian Aid, if possible. The timetable might be delayed if by doing so the participation of Christian Aid could be facilitated.

Two years prior to that there had been extensive debate amongst the Directors about pursuing the idea of an IFAT scheme for trade credit through a Clearing House. It was acknowledged that the Society would need to deal in hard currency which thus restricted it to supporting international trade. For some of the Directors involved in the organisation from inception, this meant that they had moved in their thinking of desiring to 'help the helpless' to actually feeling that the Society should target those businesses who needed credit in order to succeed in growing into strong businesses.

The debate then ranged around whether the Society should restrict itself to the fair trade movement and how appropriate it was to deal with the large northern buyers who were a part of that movement. There were differing views on whether or how fast the Society should try to work with mainstream buyers in the North.

It was recognised that the structural problems among ATOs could be for some their downfall. The view was expressed that the Society should be prepared to use its financial power and the skills of its staff in the way a merchant bank might operate to help ATOs. It was agreed that for the time being the Society should only concern itself with advising on restructurings when it was necessary to protect an existing loan.

Protecting itself against bad debts and ensuring it had sufficient liquidity to manage its portfolio suddenly started to feature on the agenda for Shared Interest. In the accounts to 30th September 1996 the general provision for bad debts was £80,000.

By the end of 1996 the Board was considering whether its policies on liquidity and lending capacity were suitable for the current lending portfolio. The policy at the time was to maintain cash reserves at 20% of instant access share capital. Mark Hayes felt that no cash reserves were necessary as they were on a six month withdrawal basis – lending tends to have a term of six months or less. And he felt the policy of restricting commitments to 80% of available capital was too conservative and commitments of 100% of available capital would be safe. He also pointed out that drawn loans would not in practice exceed the limit of 80% if the extra commitments were made.

At the same time they considered the money noted as 'social cash'. It was explained that in return for Shared Interest depositing cash with banks the banks had been persuaded to make 'soft' loans to UK development trusts. Deposits equivalent to 14% of instant access share capital were held in this way. It was agreed that all cash reserves should be held on deposit with UK banks with as much of this cash as possible linked to loans to UK development trusts.

While the discussion ranged around the money in the bank, the real issue at the time was how to get the money lent. There were a number of options open to Shared Interest. One was to offer loans at a reduced rate but Mark Hayes felt that lending by the Society was not price sensitive.

There was general agreement that a three year plan to use up the liquidity should be prepared. It was agreed that the budget in its next version should concentrate on taking up the liquidity including measures to increase the loan portfolio even if that was at the expense of some profit.

With more staff members being recruited, it was recognised that Shared Interest needed to move to new premises. New offices were sourced on Collingwood Street and on 23rd February 1998 Clare Short, then Secretary of State for International Development opened the offices. Graham Young, then General Director of Traidcraft Exchange and Chair of the Shared Interest Council, recalls this occasion with amusement: *"Shared Interest's offices were visited by Clare Short MP. Mark Hayes was explaining to her about what Shared Interest did in a rather simple way when the Secretary of State interrupted him and told him in no uncertain terms not to patronise her! Then, in the embarrassed silence which followed, told him to carry on, which, all credit to Mark, he managed to do!"*

The organisation was to enter another significant phase when in September 1997 Mark Hayes announced to the board his intention not to stand for re-election as Managing Director at the 1999 AGM. In the letter he sent to the Chair after the September board meeting, he explained his decision.

30th September 1997

Dear Chris

I spoke to you and the other directors on 17 September to advise you of my intention not to stand for re-election as Managing Director at the AGM in March 1999. I would like you all to know what this decision does, and does not, mean. It is notice of retirement from that post, not of a resignation. I remain deeply committed to Shared Interest, and indeed it is my concern for its success which prompts me to this.

I am not leaving, since I will continue at the very least as an active member. Founders of organisations are often accused of leaving their retirement too late; I may be charged with stepping down too early, and therefore some explanation is in order.

The principle reason is that Shared Interest needs, sooner rather than later, to prove that it can attract and retain a chief executive of the right calibre and on appropriate terms. The reduction of dependence on myself has always been a key objective of Board policy. Unless this can be done, Shared Interest will not be a sustainable organisation and also, my personal project will not be complete.

The skills required are changing. Less innovation, less financial engineering, more plain doggedness in pursuit of difficult but clear objectives, more personnel issues, more "management". I think another person could do a better job, though I say so cautiously, and they will certainly do it differently. There is always a risk in allowing another person to take the helm, but it is a risk we must take sooner or later.

Having made my own decision, I must tell you that a great load has come off my shoulders. I see the next 18 months as just as important, if not even more important, than any previous episode in the progress. The fact that I can see the end of the chapter, though not the book, gives me some clear targets and objectives which I am confident I can fulfil, and so leave a firm platform for my successor to build upon.

Kind regards,
yours sincerely,
Mark Hayes
Managing Director

Following Mark's announcement there was a board discussion as to how to recruit a new Managing Director with the conclusion that targeted advertising would be the best and most cost-effective way to produce results.

At the September 1998 board meeting the Board reviewed the results of the Managing Director assessment process. The application from Stephanie Sturrock was discussed and it was agreed that she was the preferred candidate for the job. Stephanie had an interesting background. After a degree in Environmental Studies, she had then taken a Masters in Technical Change and Industrial Strategy. Her career after her degrees started with local government finance where she qualified as an accountant. At the same time she was a volunteer for the credit union movement and various charities. After a while she became disenamoured with local government and was appointed General Manager of the Association of British Credit Unions (ABCUL), this was at the time when it moved its operation from London to the Co-op Union base in Manchester. It was interest in the co-operative movement that attracted Stephanie to the Shared Interest Managing Director advert. By the time she applied for the post she had been General Manager at ABCUL for two years and was looking for the opportunity to run a credit union or financial co-operative herself. The advertisement by Shared Interest was well timed and Stephanie leapt at the opportunity to lead such an interesting financial co-operative.

The interview process was very thorough Stephanie recalled. An interview panel of five Directors and a separate pre-interview meeting with Mark Hayes, who at the time made it clear that he wanted to stay around in some capacity at Shared Interest although indicated there was some opportunity to discuss his role. At the time Stephanie viewed this as a positive move, help with vision and achievement of mission but once in post, she realised it can be difficult to stamp your own mark with the founder and previous Managing Director watching your every move.

CIRSA

Comunidades Indígenas De La Región de Simojovel De Allende, Mexico. Established in 1992, CIRSA's long-term goals are to counteract poverty and the marginalisation of rural and indigenous communities

CHAPTER 5
DIFFICULT TIMES

"No one can deny that the Bridgehead episode was a testing time. Mark was valiant in his attempt to prevent the complete collapse of this Canadian buyer and he achieved his aim of ensuring producers were paid and their access to the fair trade market was protected. Of course the intention was that Shared Interest would also recoup its financial losses by steering Bridgehead out of choppy waters. This latter objective wasn't achieved, but the fact that members were kept well informed throughout the process demonstrated Shared Interest's commitment to transparency; a value that it continues to promote today."
Stephanie Sturrock, former Managing Director

With any newly established business, the early stages of growth don't always run smoothly and Shared Interest had a few difficult times in its first decade of trading. For the most part, the issues arose during Mark Hayes years as Managing Director although some of them were still ongoing after Stephanie took over the reins in November 1998.

Early on there was a problem with the Inland Revenue who struggled to classify Shared Interest. They were unsure whether Shared Interest should be classified as a trading or investment company and depending on their classification as to what their tax position should be.

While the trading versus investment company debate was going on, the majority of the Board Directors at Shared Interest were discussing whether charitable status for the fledgling organisation was desirable. Even if it was, there was some question over whether it was actually achievable bearing in mind comments received from the Inland Revenue when the Fairtrade Foundation applied for charitable status in 1994.

By August 1993 Mark had redrafted the rules of the organisation but these had been rejected by the Inland Revenue not on technical grounds but on the basic issue of poverty relief through trade. The Inland Revenue had suggested asking the Charity Commission for a ruling on this point and it was agreed that an approach would be made via the Registry of Friendly Societies who appeared sympathetic to the position of Shared Interest.

In order to pursue tax exemption as a charity with the Inland Revenue, the Inland Revenue had indicated that they would at least require the amendment of Shared Interest's entrenchment rules which would require an unopposed extraordinary resolution. As a consequence at the board meeting in August 1993 it was agreed that an interim revision to 'non-profit' status should be proposed to the Council for decision at the 1994 AGM. There was some concern from Board members that the resolution would fail, given the membership's strong feelings about the word 'charity' and the difficulty of making the case for conversion. It was hoped that Shared Interest would have a decision from the Inland Revenue once they had their reaction to the new charitable rules due hopefully in September 1993. In the end though, at the board meeting in November 1993, the Directors agreed that charitable tax status should no longer be pursued for the Society and that its tax assessment should be agreed with the Revenue.

While this appeared at the time to have concluded matters, unfortunately then in March 1994 Mark Hayes had to share with the Society's Directors that contrary to expectation and previous advice Shared Interest did now have a serious tax problem. He explained that at the January 1993 meeting the auditors had reported to the AGM that the Inland Revenue had agreed to the effect that Shared Interest was not an investment company. In May 1993, the Revenue had written to the auditors advising that they had changed their minds, but the auditors had omitted to pass this on to Shared Interest. The partner had genuinely forgotten, as subsequently evidenced by the fact that he signed the audit report on the 1993 accounts without 1992's warning on the tax position.

The hearing before the General Commissioners set for 8 April 1994 was therefore to consider whether Shared Interest was a trading or an investment company. This question was proving very complex, and although Mark Hayes remained sanguine that Shared Interest would carry the day, it would not be easy and more time was needed to prepare the case.

The Directors noted that if Shared Interest lost the tax case, there would be an immediate tax liability of some £25,000. This would significantly reduce Shared Interest's reserves in the short run. Furthermore it would undermine the entire basis of Shared Interest's operation, both in terms of the treatment of promotion costs and the deductibility of lending losses.

In July 1995, Mark Hayes was able to report that at a recent meeting with the Inland Revenue they had agreed to treat Shared Interest's accounts from 1991 onwards as those of a trading company. It had also been agreed that discounts on bills would be treated on the accruals basis rather than taking the profit into account on maturity. Two or more years after the debate had been initiated; they finally had their decision from the Inland Revenue.

The Inland Revenue wasn't the only official entity to have some queries over the status of Shared Interest. In August 1993 some correspondence between Shared Interest and the Bank of England confirmed that Shared Interest was not in breach of the Banking Act, but in the course of the correspondence Mark Hayes had discovered that the present members' loans of £32,000 were 'ultra vires' under Shared Interest's own rules, making the Directors' personally liable for them. When they discussed the matter, the Directors were content to accept the risk, provided that the rules were changed at the next AGM, and that no deposits were taken until then.

A few years later in November 1996 Mark Hayes reported to the Board on a meeting with the Bank of England which he attended with Shared Interest Board member Leonard Beighton, former Deputy Chairman of the Board of Inland Revenue and Shared Interest's solicitor Malcolm Lynch. The Bank of England considered that by issuing Loan Stock, Shared Interest might be carrying on an unauthorised deposit-taking (banking) business. The Bank had requested, and Mark had given, an undertaking that they would not release the monies subscribed for Loan Stock 2001 at least until a further meeting had taken place on 26th November.

Mark Hayes had advanced detailed arguments with the assistance of Chris Ruck, Leonard Beighton and Shared Interest's solicitors rebutting the Bank of England's allegation. He had consulted Ali Malek, QC on these arguments and the facts of the case. Counsel's opinion was not encouraging but conceded it was a difficult case and that there was force in Shared Interest's arguments.

In the light of this the Directors resolved that they would not issue further stock or release the Loan Stock 2001 funds from trust without the Bank's agreement. They further resolved that in the light of Counsel's opinion, they did not wish to test the matter in the courts. It was proposed that Mark Hayes and Leonard Beighton, advised by Shared Interest's solicitors, would seek to negotiate a compromise with the Bank and that such a compromise should allow Shared Interest to retain the monies from Loan Stock 2000 and

Loan Stock 2001 but require the Bank's agreement to any further issues.

In February 1997 the Board discussed the unfavourable response from the Bank of England. As there was much still to be resolved it was agreed that this would not be debated at the forthcoming AGM but instead they would undertake the necessary analysis and discussion so that a firm course of action could be agreed at the May board meeting.

As it happened there was an intermediary discussion at the board meeting in March when a number of papers including a draft reply to the Bank of England were discussed. Directors were asked for their comments and these varied from seeing some weakness in the Bank's opinion but nevertheless feeling that the legal battle could not be won and therefore a compromise with the bank would be the best approach. Others felt that there was nothing to be gained by "caving in" at this stage. After a wide ranging discussion it was agreed that the most conciliatory approach would be to ask for the Bank's approval of another approach to future Loan Stocks and then in trying to finesse such approval, if it could be obtained to cover Loan Stock 2001.

At the May meeting, Mark tabled a set of papers containing a letter to the Bank of England, the Bank's reply and an opinion from Counsel. He went on to explain in depth the mechanism he was proposing for a new Loan Stock 2002 into which the problematic Loan Stock 2001 could be subsumed.

The Bank of England had raised no adverse comments on the Society's proposals as set out in the letter dated 1st May 1997. Leonard Beighton thought that no more technicalities should be debated with the Bank but Mark wondered whether ceasing to argue on the legal point was in the Society's best interests. There was some debate as to how the new proposal would be presented to the holders of Loan Stock 2001 and it was suggested that if the proposal was accepted then an effort should be made to complete the new Loan Stock Issue by the end of November 1997.

It was agreed to proceed on the basis outlined i.e. the issue should take place at the end of November 1997 if possible and a full disclosure of the situation to be made to the Co-operative Bank by Mark Hayes and it would be presented to members that a technical problem had been overcome by a formula discussed with the Bank of England.

The Moderator then raised the practical point of whether the documentation for Loan Stock 2002 should be settled by a lawyer. Mark thought that an opinion from Malcolm Lynch and an approach to the Bank of England with a draft of the offer documents should be enough to overcome concerns. This was agreed and the matter was concluded.

This was not long before Shared Interest challenged conventional thinking among regulators about what constituted a deposit. In May 1999, HM Treasury published a consultation document on withdrawable share capital. Withdrawable share capital was at the very heart of the cooperative movement and the basis on which Shared Interest was able to take members funds and lend them in a very direct way at risk. A key part of Shared Interest's 'contract' with its members is the understanding that members could lose some or all of their investment. However other parts of the cooperative movement were considering a way of 'protecting' members funds, in a similar way that bank deposits are protected by regulation. The introduction of a compulsory deposit protection regime for all withdrawable share capital would have threatened Shared Interest's very existence. With the support of Malcolm Lynch Solicitors, Counsel's opinion was sought and although not conclusive, it convinced the Board that the there was a strong case to be made.

Following extensive lobbying through Co-operatives UK, including a meeting with their Chief Executive, Dame Pauline Green, and HM Treasury itself, it was clear that Shared Interest was the largest among a small group of social finance organisations affected by this proposal.

Stephanie Sturrock recalls: *"It was not until HM Treasury published its*

report 'Enterprise and Social Exclusion' (known as PAT3 Report) in November
1999 that its position finally became clear. We had proved our point and
defended our ability to make 'risky' loans with people's share capital to people
in poorer parts of the world."

3.70 A number of CFIs (Community Finance Institutions) are registered
as Industrial and Provident Societies (I&Ps). HMT issued a consultation
document in May 1999 about the exemption from the Banking Act
for Withdrawable Share Capital (WSC). The document said that it
seemed likely that most (if not all) issuance of WSC would fall under
the definition of deposit. As a result of the consultation, it has become
clear that the terms on which WSC is issued varies considerably, and
does not necessarily always involve the issuance of deposits. For the
avoidance of doubt, HMT, having consulted the FSA, wishes to make it
clear that withdrawable shares will represent deposits only if the sums
involved are paid on terms which provide for their repayment in full.
Where withdrawable shares do not constitute deposits, societies will
not be affected by the changes proposed, since they have no need to
rely on the exemption.

While these two ongoing debates with the Inland Revenue and the Bank of
England were significant at the time, the challenge that many recall as the
most difficult time for Shared Interest was the failure of Bridgehead, the fair
trade subsidiary of Oxfam Canada.

As Roger Sawtell, Council Moderator, recalled: *"At one stage, as Moderator*
of Council, I thought the major failure of a Canadian venture, hardly a
developing country, might sink us, but in those early years, the remarkable

feature to me was the relatively small number of failures to repay loans. The carefully-judged lending procedures were a firm foundation on which the subsequent growth of Shared Interest was built."

The failure of Bridgehead received significant coverage in Quarterly Return as the Directors and staff at Shared Interest attempted to convey to the members the issues around the largest loss Shared Interest has suffered in its twenty year history.

Shared Interest first detailed its link with Bridgehead in the third issue of Quarterly Return in November 1991 when it announced it was Shared Interest's first direct loan independent of EDCS. The loan was for £40,000. The relationship with Bridgehead continued until 1996, when Mark Hayes, having heard it had made a loss of Canadian $1m, first went out to visit it. Upon his return the Board was asked to approve a revised application from Bridgehead, whose difficulties had not yet been resolved, for a facility of the order of $150,000 (US).

Early in 1997 Mark then explained to the Board of Shared Interest that two rescue plans had been attempted and the latest rescue plan seemed to be succeeding under the influence of Michel Beauregard, the Chief Financial Officer. To support this rescue plan an increased facility of $450,000 (US) was recommended by Mark to the Board although it was noted by Chris Ruck, as Moderator that the size of the facility was more than the Society's reserves. Some concern was expressed about lending to an insolvent company but Mark emphasised the short term nature of the facility and thought it would be perverse not to lend in this financial year after Bridgehead seemed to have turned the corner and the rescue looked likely to succeed. After the views of all the Directors had been considered the proposed credit facility was agreed.

However by the end of 1997, the situation was not looking good as Bridgehead filed for protection from its creditors on 31st December 1997. At the time though, Mark Hayes and Colin Crawford expressed the opinion that they thought there was still a viable business there which could be rescued. Just a few months later, Mark explained to the Board that all the bids for the company had been rejected and an attempt to continue to trade would be made. This might lead to a request for further finance. If the Society were to provide this finance then a scheme for repayment of the failed loan would be a precondition.

A month later an urgent board meeting was called at Shared Interest to discuss Mark's proposal for the Society to continue to support Bridgehead by taking control of the organisation through a trust designed to protect the producers who would otherwise not be paid. There was then much debate about what issues would need to be overcome if the Society was to continue to discuss the option of taking control as Mark was proposing. Some felt that it was not the role of Shared Interest to assist and that there were other Canadian or US ATOs who should step in rather than the Society try to run things from a distance. There was a real concern about the amount of management time that would be needed to be invested into this which would slow down development in other areas.

At a board meeting in April 1998 Mark summarised the main points in his paper 'Bridgehead Strategy and Tactics' which were that the loan to Bridgehead of £222,100 had been lost and this loss to the Society was as a result of mistakes by Bridgehead and an over reliance by the Society on assurances based on faulty figures. It was recognised that this would have a severe impact on the lending loss reserve and that the Society's strategy could be called into question as repeated losses of this magnitude would be unsustainable.

The discussion which followed concentrated on the value of the assets of Bridgehead which would be acquired. Tracey Clark, Managing Director at Bridgehead then presented Directors with a paper, 'The case for acquiring

Bridgehead' and gave a talk illustrating her paper. In response to questions from Directors she explained how the financial figures had been so badly misrepresented during 1997, and her own role in bringing matters to a head. Tracey expressed her personal confidence in her ability to carry out the plan she was proposing and confirmed her favourable view of the middle management which was now in place at Bridgehead.

There was much discussion following these two papers and the outcome was published in a Bridgehead supplement, which went out shortly after Quarterly Return Issue 27 in the Spring of 1998. It was recognised there was a need to keep members fully informed if the rescue went ahead:

How much is at stake?
The amount in question is about £220,000, which is less than our current reserve for lending losses of £260,000, but which would nevertheless be a severe loss. When formulating our policy on lending losses, we envisaged losses on lending to producer organisations, which for one reason or another had been unable to fulfil the orders placed with them by fair trade buyers. We had not seriously expected major defaults on the part of the buyers themselves, particularly subsidiaries of members of OXFAM International, since we are able to monitor their financial position more easily. In this case the financial information available to Bridgehead substantially misrepresented their true position.

A further issue is that producer organisations are owed about £70,000 by Bridgehead which they stand to lose.

Resolution
On 17th April 1998 the Directors of Shared Interest approved a

proposal under which the business and assets of Bridgehead will be transferred to a new subsidiary company owned by Shared Interest, in effect accepting those trading assets (book value about £400,000) in exchange for our £220,000.

At the same time we agreed to provide a further £300,000 in normal trade credit to cover orders for producer organisations. We will also pay the outstanding £70,000 owed to producer organisations, although we intend to recover this from the OXFAMs. Another fair trade buyer has underwritten this sum in case the OXFAMs do not pay – it was a requirement on our part that the producer organisations should be paid in full without risk to us.

The new Bridgehead will be led by a new Managing Director, Tracey Clark, a Canadian with the necessary skills and commitment to make a success of Bridgehead, including an MBA as well as a year's work with Bangladesh Rural Advancement Committee (BRAC), a major producer organisation. Tracey will report to the Shared Interest Board.

Mark Hayes, Managing Director, 1st May 1998

In May 1998 it became clear that Shared Interest's decision to attempt to rescue Bridgehead was not a decision supported by EDCS, who also part-financed Bridgehead and were also likely to lose significant amounts of money. With the benefit of hindsight, EDCS's decision was right to not support the rescue attempt but at the time there was great disappointment on the part of Shared Interest that EDCS were unsupportive of their proposal and it was proposed that two Shared Interest Directors should meet with the General Manager of EDCS to attempt to restore the relationship with them.

Quarterly Return 28, summer 1998 gave an update:

You will have received a supplement after your last Quarterly Return, telling you of developments with the Canadian fair trading company Bridgehead.

We had to delay the sending out of this supplement, as the whole thing was complicated by innumerable legal difficulties, and for a number of weeks our proposal hung in the balance. These difficulties have now been ironed out and the proposal went through on 18th June.

We have now repaid all those producer groups who were owed money by Bridgehead and they, and Bridgehead are now able to continue trading.

Producer responds:
"This is big good news that Shared Interest Society has taken over Bridgehead 1998 Inc and all the standing money of the producers is being paid.

"Thankfully we have received our money already on 27th June. This is a big relief to our producer groups.

"Tara Projects stands for a definite security of the producers' money and therefore we also deserve security of our payments. Shared Interest has done a great job in this direction."
Shyam S.Sharma, Tara Projects

In Quarterly Return Issue 29 published in the autumn of 1998, some of the more critical members' letters were published although it was noted at the time that most letters received from members had been supportive:

With the action you have taken, you have more than doubled the exposure of Shared Interest to Bridgehead. This is a very bold decision. In addition, you've made Bridgehead a subsidiary. If future problems arise in trading, what will Shared Interest's liabilities be?

Mark Hayes replies: *"Since Bridgehead is now controlled by us we have a moral, if not legal, responsibility for any further losses. On the other hand we have the opportunity to earn back our £220,000 loss, and indeed more. This was an exceptional measure to deal with what we hope was an exceptional problem."*

————

We are shoring up a failing ATO and, in effect, cushioning producers from the real world. What help is that in the long term to either of them? I would rather see Shared Interest go down a different route. Can we have a think tank on microcredit please?

————

I consider very definitely that if Bridgehead was in difficulties, Oxfam should have 'bailed them out' as they are such a large organisation.

————

I am sure it is right, where possible, to extricate Third World producer organisations from their connections with a company which is going bankrupt, at no loss to them. Our organisation should not though, turn itself into a kind of Seventh Cavalry for Alternative Trading companies in trouble, at least not with any regularity.

————

What you have done is a reasonable risk to take and the best thing to do under the circumstances. The main thing is that the producer groups should be paid.

———

I would like to congratulate the Board on finding a solution to the Bridgehead problem which ensures that Third World producers do not suffer because of mismanagement in an Oxfam group subsidiary.

In Quarterly Return, published in the winter of 1998, cautious optimism about the future of Bridgehead was expressed:

As members know, in June 1998 we took over the business of Bridgehead in Canada.

Over the next two years we expect to sell Bridgehead to a Fair Trade consumer cooperative formed for the purpose, and which is launched this spring. The customer response to the idea has been enthusiastic. It may take that long for the trading recovery of the business to be consolidated, for the coop Board to be formed, for capital to be raised and for a purchase agreement to be negotiated. However, at this stage we can be cautiously optimistic.

However by the middle of 1999, it looked like the optimism expressed six months before was premature as the plans for a cooperative had not yet been launched and by the autumn of 1999 no approaches had been made by other ATOs to take on any aspects of the business. Towards the end of the year it then became a question for Shared Interest as to whether to continue to invest or withdraw and in Quarterly Return in the winter of 1999, failure was announced:

Members may recall that we last reported on this a year ago when we had just dealt with the results of its insolvency and a period of painful reorganisation. At that time we were optimistic that we could get the business back up on its feet and eventually transfer it to a consumer cooperative formed for the purpose. We had three main objectives when we took on this business: to ensure producers did not lose any money; to ensure producers' access to the Canadian fair trade market was protected and if possible, to recoup some of our losses, without any further losses.

In all we met our first objective, substantially met the second, but did not meet the third. We protected producers' businesses and partially their market but in the process the Society has suffered costs.

At the March 2000 board meeting, Mark explained his intention to report to the AGM that the Bridgehead venture had been a defeat. At the May 2000 meeting Mark reported that Bridgehead was now dissolved although the final payment had not yet been received. If all went as expected the further and final provision should be for no more than £30,000.

In the last piece to members on the matter, a Bridgehead post mortem was published in Quarterly Return in the spring of 2000:

At the AGM we also took a hard look at the failure of one of the fair trade buyers, Bridgehead in Canada.

Members will also remember that we took this company over two years ago in an attempt to rescue it. In the last QR we reported that it had been decided to close it down.

Mark Hayes, who became the Chair of the Board of Bridgehead when we took it over, explained to members that when all the accounts had been finalised, we had lost more than we thought. As he said, this is a defeat, and with hindsight maybe it would have been better not to get involved. We did it of course to help those producers who stood to lose what Bridgehead owed them. However would it have been cheaper to simply pay those producers off? Maybe but the reality is of course that at the time we did not have the benefit of hindsight, and also it was not our place to pay Bridgehead's debts. We could only help by intervening and giving Bridgehead a chance to trade its way out of difficulty. In the end this turned out not to be possible.

In asking, if it was money well-spent, we can say that yes, for the producers who would have suffered or even gone under when Bridgehead failed in 1998, and for all those who have been sustained by Bridgehead's orders in the last two years, it was well spent. But from our members' point of view, we can only apologise for these losses.

While one member thanked the Board for their response to Bridgehead, saying it had been handled as well as it could have been, another warned against having subsidiaries and asked why, as Bridgehead had been an Oxfam subsidiary, Oxfam had not come to the rescue.

All were grateful to Mark for his openness about it.

NARANJILLO

Established by 32 founder members almost 50 years ago, this coffee and cocoa producer organisation from Peru was established as a way to fight against the middle men who paid low prices for their products

CHAPTER 6

LAUNCHING THE

CLEARING HOUSE

"Shared Interest has a very special and symbiotic relationship with the Fair Trade movement and IFAT in particular. A major benefit of IFAT membership is eligibility to join the Clearing House scheme and access other Shared Interest credit facilities. This is hugely appreciated in many developing countries where obtaining credit is difficult and expensive. The difference between Shared Interest and other financial institutions is that Shared Interest works exclusively with Fair Trade organisations and so is able to focus 100% on the financial challenges they face. A dedicated team of Shared Interest staff spend much of the working year visiting IFAT members, wherever they are in the world, and running workshops at IFAT meetings to explain the services that are on offer."

Carol Wills, Executive Director of IFAT. (Shared Interest 2002 Annual Report)

Some of the larger US fair trade organisations have in 2008/2009 celebrated 60 years of buying and selling fair trade goods. Although they started their work in the 1940s, fair trade organisations around the world only began to meet together from the mid 1970s. Their meetings were usually informal conferences every couple of years. By the mid 1980s there was a desire to come together more formally and towards the end of the decade, in 1987 the European Fair Trade Association (EFTA) was established. EFTA is an association of the 11 largest importing organisations in Europe. The International Federation for Alternative Trade (IFAT), now the World Fair Trade Organisation (WFTO) was established in 1989. The heads of FLO (Fairtrade Labelling Organisation), WFTO, NEWS! (Network of European World Shops) and EFTA started to meet together in 1998 so as to enable these networks and their members to cooperate on important areas of work, such as advocacy and campaigning, standards and monitoring of fair trade.

Shared Interest early on established a close relationship with the World Fair Trade Organisation (WFTO) known then as the International Federation for Alternative Trade (IFAT). Of the networks mentioned above WFTO is the only global network whose members represent the fair trade chain from production to sale. It is a significant network with an international membership of 436 organisations, all of whom are fully committed to fair trade. WFTO now operates across 5 regions of the globe: Africa, Asia, Europe, Latin America, and North America and the Pacific Rim. Each region has its own board and they feed into an elected global board. As a fair trade network it aims to create market access through policy, advocacy, campaigning, marketing and monitoring.

This close relationship was to become particularly significant in the late 1990s when Shared Interest began to establish its new method of lending, the Clearing House. In the Spring of 1997 Mark Hayes and Colin Crawford had attended the IFAT biennial conference in Southern India and presented to all the participants the proposal that Shared Interest act as a clearing house for trade finance for members. It was emphasised that this would empower producers who would be able to sell to any IFAT buyer and still have access to credit from the Clearing House. It was also made clear that both buyers and producers would benefit as payments would be consolidated cutting down on bank charges. The proposal was greeted enthusiastically at the time by IFAT members.

The strategic partnership that Shared Interest established at the time with what was then known as IFAT, gave the title to the lending system – the Shared Interest IFAT Clearing House. It was agreed between the two organisations that only members of IFAT would be able to access credit via the Shared Interest IFAT Clearing House. In doing this Shared Interest hoped to do its bit to strengthen the global network of IFAT and at the same time, membership of IFAT allowed Shared Interest not to be diverted by assessing individual organisations' fair trade credentials as this was a requirement of their IFAT membership.

This decision to set up the Clearing House led to a piece in Quarterly Return in the summer of 1998 called 'Dealing with Risk':

Shared Interest's decision to set up a Clearing House for the International Federation for Alternative Trade (IFAT) coupled with the lending losses made last year and the Bridgehead drama have combined to make the Board consider again the issue of risk.

It has become clearer that, as the IFAT Clearing House allows us to get closer to Third World producers, and to lend to them more directly, so the possibility of losses increases. Similarly, it has become clearer through the Bridgehead situation that even the First World buyers are not necessarily secure investment.

The Board believe that, while we must have – and do have – good systems in place for making lending decisions and for monitoring our loans, we cannot do our business properly without involving the possibility of loss. If we are to reach people whom the banks can't or won't, because they don't have security which they can pledge, there is inevitably a risk of losses. And the losses could be of a scale which would more than wipe out our reserves so that we would have to make a charge on members' share capital.

I am sorry to say that Bill Midgley, who until his very recent retirement was the Chief Executive of Newcastle Building Society and who joined the Shared Interest Board in January 1998, is unable to support this view and has decided to resign. He believes that the Society should not put its members' savings at risk in this way and hence our investment policy has to be designed to reduce the degree of risk very significantly. He does not want to be a member of a divided Board and since the rest of the Board are unanimous on this point, he believes that the best course is to withdraw now. We are very sorry to see him go as, even in the short time he has been with us, it was clear that he had much to contribute to our deliberations.

The possibility of a charge on capital is spelled out in the current investment booklet, as it was in previous versions. However in order to be sure that there can be no misunderstanding, we have reprinted the booklet to make the position even clearer. We are enclosing with this issue of Quarterly Return a copy of the new booklet so that every existing member has an opportunity to see what we are saying about the risks. We hope that after reading it every member will feel able to continue to take the risks which we believe to be inherent in our mission of lending for the benefit of poor people in the Developing

World so that they can earn a better living for themselves and their families.

However, let there be no doubt. If after reading the booklet, you are, like Bill Midgley, uncomfortable with our approach, now is the time to withdraw. We shall be sorry to see anyone go, but we have adequate funds from which to pay out those who wish to leave.

A year later a similar issue arose when the Board reviewed the Society's lending policy. Mark had proposed a number of points for discussion upon which Roger Salmon another former banker had written to all Board members setting out his view that parts of the lending policy would, if persevered with, result in an unacceptably high risk of losses. Roger went on to state that he would find it difficult to continue as a Director if in his view the risk of losses was too great.

There was a wide ranging discussion which the Moderator, Leonard Beighton attempted to summarise by asking the board members to consider the question: *"Is the lending policy broadly correct assuming that its implications are spelt out fully to members?"* Each of the Board members except Roger Salmon replied in the positive.

Shared Interest did not generally take security and in its lending took a quasi equity position, normally ranking behind other lenders. This was against the natural instinct of bankers, who wanted to see lending secured in some way. When Bill and Roger finally left the Board, Shared Interest took the view that the sort of senior financial figure they needed on the Board was a venture capitalist who was comfortable with assessing investments on the basis of future business success and the qualities of management rather than availability of security. Soon after, Shared Interest recruited

Michael Walton.

Roger Salmon's departure was openly reported in Quarterly Return, reproducing his resignation letter citing the main reasons as what he regarded to be *"equity risks in loans to buyers"* and *"unquantifiable risks in loans to producers"*. The article went on to reassure members that all other Directors were confident that a proper account of risks had consistently been given to members.

It is commonly acknowledged that although Mark Hayes during his time as Managing Director, did much to develop and create the Clearing House, it was Stephanie Sturrock during her time as Managing Director who actually got the Clearing House up and running. It was with her leadership that the staff team engaged with and brought on board many of the larger fair trade buyer organisations. By consolidating their orders, through the Clearing House, the producer organisations that they worked with were also able to independently access credit at a blanket interest rate of 4% over Shared Interest's prime rate.

How the Clearing House system works
Shared Interest has created a Clearing House, which allows the consolidation of orders from fair trade buyers to fair trade producers. It also enables producers to access additional credit independently from the buyers. The diagram below shows how an individual order for goods is financed but, in reality, many such orders are being processed at any one time.

1. A Clearing House buyer places an order with a producer.
2. Shared Interest makes an advance payment to the producer, on

behalf of the buyer, usually 50% of the value of the order.

3. If the producer organisation is a Clearing House member it can borrow an additional amount (30% of the value of the order) as 'export credit' against that order. If a buyer cannot afford to make an advance payment then the producer can borrow up to 80% of the value of the order.

4. Once the goods have been made and packed, the producer sends them to the buyer.

5. The final payment is made to the producer by Shared Interest (upon the instruction of the buyer), net of any export credit and interest owed by the producer against that order.

6. The buyer then has a period of credit during which to sell the goods. The buyer then pays back Shared Interest the full value of the goods plus interest incurred during the whole credit period.

The Clearing House

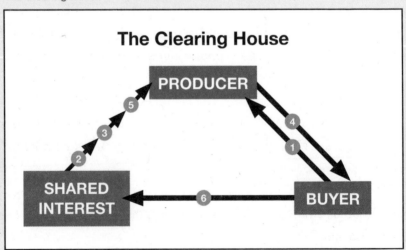

Stephanie took up the position of Managing Director in November 1998 and was welcomed by Leonard Beighton, then Moderator of the Board. The Moderator of the Board confirmed that the business that Mark had created and established had a significant share capital base and the capital was continuing to come in but the main task for Stephanie would be to get the money lent out. Of course, as detailed in the previous chapter, Stephanie was joining the organisation at a tumultuous time. Bridgehead was very much on the agenda with the discussion at the time around whether or not to take it over. Stephanie recalled this was very distracting in those early days, not least as she visited Bridgehead very early on with Mark Hayes who was now in post as Deputy Moderator (Executive).

Bridgehead aside, overall Stephanie's impression of the organisation she had taken over the leadership of, was very positive. Stephanie recalls: *"I was very impressed with the Board, the quality of debate and the depth of discussion and I was similarly impressed with the concept and activities of the Council."* It was around this time that the Council had brought to the AGM the suggestion that 4 of the 9 Council members should be randomly selected from the membership – a process similar to the jury system but without the element of compulsion! This process was adopted with enthusiasm as Ian Baird-Smith one of the first four randomly selected Council members later describes:

"Sometime before Christmas a letter dropped on my mat from Shared Interest. The new method of electing four Council members at random from the membership list had found my name.

"My initial reaction was 'I don't have time for this'. However as I thought about the idea and reread the letter I realized that this was something I actually wanted to do and so the enthusiasm grew

"In preparation for our election we were booked on a training day at the

beginning of February. The Saturday morning dawned bright and sunny and we all assembled in time to cross to St Mary's Island, east of Newcastle before the tide came up at 10.45. All four of us new recruits to Council, together with several existing Council member and new Board members, were isolated in St Mary's lighthouse until the afternoon when the tide receded enough for us to cross to the mainland.

"The intervening five hours passed like lightning as we learned about the basis of Shared Interest, the purpose of lending to Third World producer and how Shared Interest fits into the fair trade system.

"Altogether it was a most enjoyable way of getting to know the other Council and Board members and especially being able to grasp the vision of Shared Interest as a way for us in the material 90s to help those in the Third World who are trying to help themselves."
(Quarterly Return issue 27, Spring 1998)

Roger Sawtell also recalled this change to the Council: *"One of the unusual organisational features of the Council was the introduction of 'random nomination' of some Council members from the growing list of investing members. Grey-haired folk told us that randomly nominated Council members would not agree to serve, but that was not the case and, for example, I remain in touch with a relatively young randomly nominated Council member who benefited from the unexpected experience."*

· What impressed Stephanie the most when she joined the organisation was Mark's clear vision for the way forward. The concept of the Clearing House was brilliant although he still had some work to do to get others externally to fully understand and as a consequence support the idea. Internally, when Mark had outlined his idea for the Clearing House some Board members had questioned whether IFAT would be flooded with applications from coffee cooperatives. Over 80% of the fair trade market at the time was in coffee but

IFAT's membership was very craft orientated and applications from coffee producers keen to access finance could imbalance the organisation. It was agreed that by putting a commodity limit in place this would protect the Society against the risk of the scheme being overwhelmed by traders in one commodity. As a consequence Mark when he presented the Clearing House proposal to IFAT members referred to the likelihood of both commodity and sector limits. It was also agreed that the current lending loss reserve of 5% of share capital might be insufficient although it was hoped with a wider spread of borrowers that the overall risk would be reduced.

These discussions about risk were a fundamental part of a growing organisation and were expanded on during a discussion at a Board meeting towards the end of 1999. Performance risk was discussed first with the risk represented by failure to deliver. Those with direct experience of the fair trade market, indicated that special circumstances exist and the dynamic is producer orientated and a great deal of teamwork is applied to solving delivery problems. The risk of failure to deliver is factored into the system, which seems sufficiently resilient to deal with it. Buyers do not, typically, get into problems because of late or incomplete delivery. It was therefore agreed that performance risk on buyer credits was relatively low.

Producer risk was discussed next and it was noted that producers tend to be conservative, risk-averse organisations. It was felt that the Society's risk would reduce further as it developed a portfolio of small loans direct with many producers well spread throughout the world rather than the present fewer, larger facilities.

Commodity risk was noted as worthy of discussion and the discussion focused in particular on coffee as that was the commodity in respect of which the Society had reached its commodity limit. There was a discussion about the fair trade pricing of coffee. The practice of setting commodity limits was confirmed and a discussion about whether the present limit of 10%

was appropriate developed. A higher limit would allow more lending into coffee and hence more drawings. It was suggested that this would make the presentation of the Society's results more acceptable to members. However, higher risk would be incurred if a higher limit were to be agreed. In the end, no change to the limit was proposed. Lastly, sector risk was touched on although this risk it was noted was ameliorated by the geographical spread of the business.

While these discussions around risk were of course necessary and appropriate, the detail of establishing the Clearing House fell to the staff at Shared Interest and the enormous amount of effort that went into creating the relevant IT systems to support the Clearing House is worthy of note. As it was impossible to find anything suitable externally, the IT systems used were built internally, which allowed them to be designed accurately to the specification drawn up by staff after consultation with customers.

With Stephanie focusing on the lending side of the operation when she started as Managing Director, within six months she was reporting to the Board that there had been a slowdown in the rate of increase in investment. This had been a direct result of her policy of cutting down on promotion expenditure and focusing more resources on the lending side of the business. A year later with the Clearing House established and gaining momentum, Stephanie proposed initiating some limited targeted promotional activity to reverse the trend of declining membership numbers and share capital. Stephanie knew that without an increasing membership base and capital, it would be difficult to maintain the present expense ratio. Stephanie's proposal was to strengthen the Representatives Scheme and this was followed up in Quarterly Return with a request for Reps in areas of the country not covered at the time. While the Reps Scheme was being developed, it was proposed not for the time being to divert any resources to advertising or promotion whilst the great excess of unused share capital remained.

With Stephanie increasingly taking on the reins of the organisation, the Board debated the plans for Mark's role. Initially it was clearly useful to have the founder and previous Managing Director on hand to provide advice and information, but it was also inevitable that Mark needed to step away and clarify his role in order that Stephanie could operate effectively as Managing Director. At the time it was proposed that Mark would take on the role of Deputy Moderator.

Within a year of Stephanie Sturrock taking over as Managing Director, the drawn figure (so the amount actually lent) was up to 48% of lending capacity but perhaps even more exciting than that figure, was the fact that producer facilities were also beginning to be drawn. By that time nine producers had made drawings totalling £57,000.

Quarterly Return in the winter of 1999 reported on one of the new Clearing House members in Kenya, Undugu:

Undugu, Swahili for 'brotherhood', is the name of a Society set up in 1973 by a priest, Father Arnold Grol in response to the plight of street children in Nairobi.

This continues today to be the main mission of Undugu, in a city where there are some 60,000 children living on these streets. These numbers are rising as unemployment hits more and more families and the number of orphans is growing through AIDS. Although Undugu is now a large organisation with more functions than street children work, their mission is reflected in a rule that everyone in the organisation, even the Managing Director, must spend some evenings on the street befriending the street children.

Once children have got to know workers on the street they can come voluntarily to the reception centre. At the boys' centre we visited, two social workers live in with them and deal with the immense social problems experienced by these children. This task was not made easier by the fact that the centre, built to house 20 boys, had 53 boys in it; they don't want to turn any of them away.

From working in the streets, Undugu began to work in the slums, trying to prevent the conditions which drove the children to life on the streets. They work with the youth, giving training in informal sector businesses and recreational activity to counter the problem of drugs, which in turn lead to crime as the young people steal to feed their habit.

They also give business advice and run a credit scheme in the slums. Their aim is to help people to help themselves. For those who need it they give help with marketing and in some cases with exporting of their goods – and this is where our credit is needed.

As drawings continued to slowly increase over the next couple of years, it was recognised that there were definite trends in peak drawings during the course of the year with clear seasonal demands for finance. With producer drawings still continuing to be relatively low, an assessment was made of the producer market.

It was recognised that for many producers sourcing an export market can be incredibly difficult and sourcing finance to support any export order even harder. As a consequence in January 2000 a proposal for an Emerging Producer scheme limited to $100,000 was approved. This was to allow those producers that were starting out, a 'lift up' by offering them a credit facility. The limit of any one facility was agreed to be $10,000 initially and once the

$100,000 limit had been reached the overall scheme would be reviewed by the Board. As well as offering an Emerging Producer scheme, staff at Shared Interest also recognised that for many producers a term loan (rather than export credit) would be a more helpful financial product. Again a proposal went to the Board and an initial limit of $20,000 per loan subject to an overall maximum for the pilot scheme of $50,000 was agreed. In order to facilitate repayment, it was agreed that only those producers with a sufficient flow of orders through the Clearing House should be considered for term loans and that the maximum limit of loan available would be 15% of a producer's last 12 months' worth of payments received through the Clearing House from buyers.

One of the first organisations to successfully access this new term loan was Holyland Handicrafts Co-operative, a Palestinian group making olive wood products. This loan enabled them to buy wood direct from farmers when trees were pruned at the end of the olive season, both cutting out the middlemen who charged higher rates, and also guaranteeing sufficient supply for a year's worth of orders.

With share capital still sat in the bank, Stephanie raised with the Board a proposal to accept reduced returns from Social Banks in order to maintain the level of the Society's deposits with the Banks. The Society's established policy at the time was to try to earn a social return on 100% of the members' funds. As, by Board policy, 20% was kept in reserve so that members' withdrawals could be accommodated, the Social Banks provided a reliable route for these funds although not always necessarily at the most attractive interest rates. It was agreed to accept Stephanie's proposal that the money would be retained in Social Banks as long as a rate of no less than 1% below the normal Co-operative Bank rate was maintained.

The discussion over interest rates at the Social Banks led to a broader discussion of interest rate policy and the implications of lower interest rates in general. It was discussed as to whether there should be a minimum interest rate for investors and should there be a mechanistic method of setting interest rates? The conclusion was that the present Board discretion about interest rates should be retained. It was further agreed that 1% should be the minimum rate to investors.

By the summer of 2000 although growth in lending through the Clearing House had been evident, it was recognised that in order to truly realise the Society's Vision, Mission and Values and the three year plan to increase trade lending to £15m, that other financial products or ideas would need to be pursued. Various ideas were discussed including financing interATO trade, supporting producers with orders from non IFAT buyers and developing a charitable arm.

It is a reality of the fair trade movement that many of the fair trade buyer organisations source products from other buyers. This is for a variety of reasons including saving costs and allowing buyers to retain very clear relationships with their chosen producers. This interATO trade in 2000 accounted for approximately £13m of the £72m fair trade turnover. The proposal to provide finance to support this form of trade was agreed as long as it was only offered for trade between IFAT members.

The other idea that was discussed was to support producers with orders from non IFAT buyers. Quarterly Return in the winter of 2000 reported on the first loan to a producer to assist with a non IFAT buyer order:

While visiting the Undugu Society of Kenya, we were fortunate to meet David Mochama Ombasa, one of the soapstone carvers from Kisii. He was at the Undugu office collecting the advance payment we had sent to start production on a large order Undugu had received from a commercial buyer.

This is the first advance we have made of this kind, to a producer member of the Clearing House for an order from a non IFAT buyer. The decision to consider advance payments for commercial orders, on a case by case basis, came after approaches from several producers we work with. They were getting some commercial orders which they couldn't accept because there was no prepayment to finance the production of the order. It was good to see our first advance of this kind in action.

One area of the globe though that continued to defeat Shared Interest in its desire to offer credit to producers worldwide was the region of India and Bangladesh. Due to exchange controls it was not possible and continues to not be possible to operate the Clearing House in India or Bangladesh. Shared Interest was able to make payments to producers in both of these countries but could not offer credit on orders from buyers.

Various options were continually being explored. In 2000 the option of setting up a subsidiary in India was considered and researched by Colin Crawford and Jan Simmonds, Board Director during a visit to India. While this offered a solution of sorts, it was recognised that there were substantial difficulties with this approach and at the time they were felt to be beyond the capacity of the Society.

Options were also considered in Bangladesh and some considerable amount of time was invested looking into this during 2000-2002. In May 2002 Colin Crawford and Malcolm Curtis reported to the Board after they had conducted a seminar with producers in Bangladesh. Most of the organisations that attended did not have sufficient capital to subscribe to a possible mutual guarantee scheme which was the primary option being considered at the time. The producers present preferred instead the option of setting up a financial organisation within Bangladesh. Once again though, it was recognised by Shared Interest that this was not viable as a commercial undertaking although it might sit in the future more comfortably within a charitable framework.

While considering its own lending portfolio Shared Interest was also looking again at its relationship with EDCS, its strategic partner from the outset. Any earlier ill feeling against Shared Interest by EDCS over Bridgehead seemed to have now evaporated and indeed relations between the EDCS Board and its support associations also seemed to have improved. EDCS or Oikocredit as it was now known communicated to Shared Interest in the summer of 2001 that it was keen to set up its own support association in the UK. This came at a time when Shared Interest was once again considering how appropriate it was to continue the Society's support at the current levels.

For Shared Interest the news that Oikocredit hoped to establish a support association in the UK was welcomed. If it should happen, it would remove the need for the Society to offer microcredit bonds in the future. It was proposed that the Society should offer to help Oikocredit to develop its role with churches and other funders in the UK, possibly resulting in another Industrial and Provident Society being formed.

In the summer of 2001, Gert Maanen, General Manager of Oikocredit retired. He was succeeded by Tor Gull, an experienced banker from Finland, with a solid background in development work. Prior to his retirement, Gert was invited to attend Shared Interest's AGM in London in March 2001 and he spoke movingly at the AGM of the lessons we can learn from the people we help, especially from their sheer ability to survive in situations where we couldn't.

In one of the last speeches made by Gert as General Manager of Oikocredit he described the organisation he was leaving behind and explained some of the current challenges the organisation was facing:

"Our formula has proved successful; less than 10% of the loans given had to be written off. However during the last years, various natural disasters like Hurricane Mitch and the economic crisis in South East Asia, confronted us with many problems. For instance, we learned that in some countries like Indonesia, hard currency loans alone present a problem. Oikocredit is therefore faced with some major challenges and we are actively looking for new solutions, such as Local Currency Risk Funds, to guarantee that we remain an effective and relevant instrument for development in the new millennium."
(Quarterly Return, Issue 42, Winter 2002)

Changes were also afoot on the Board of Shared Interest. At the March 1998 Board meeting Chris Ruck ended his final term of office as the first Moderator of the Society. He thanked all the Board members who had made his time on the Board memorable and rewarding. He was warmly thanked for his contribution to the growth and development of the Society.

The second Moderator of the Board was Leonard Beighton and he had a shorter term of office as Moderator, stepping down in 2001. Geoff Moore was proposed as the next Moderator with the suggestion he take on the post until his retirement from the Board. Geoff Moore was unanimously voted to the post but felt because of work commitments he could not take it on fully until October 2001 but until then he would work in partnership with Leonard Beighton on a basis to be agreed.

Also in 2001, Mark Hayes, founder and first Managing Director, finally left the Board after more than a decade. The Board thanked Mark for all his contributions and confirmed how much the Society would miss him.

By November 2001 Shared Interest was faced with a new phenomenon. With the UK base rate anticipated to drop to 4% or below and likely to remain low for at least 2 years, Stephanie was clear that Shared Interest needed to change its interest rate policy. With the expense ratio at about 3.75% of share capital at the time, she strongly proposed to reduce interest rates to members with immediate effect. This was significant as she was calling on the Board to abandon its previous policy of a 1% minimum interest rate on share capital. The Board agreed to set a revised minimum interest rate of 0% while noting that the Society's rules did not allow a negative interest rate. It was agreed that interest to members would be at a rate of 0% from 1st December 2001.

While provisions were being made for low interest rates in the future, it was acknowledged that for the time being Shared Interest at least was profitable and towards the end of 2001, there was a discussion by the Board on how to use the surplus made by the Society.

This was discussed in Quarterly Return in the Autumn of 2001 in an article called 'Spending our surplus':

One of the most telling things about any organisation is what it does with the profit it makes. Shared Interest has made a profit each year and has provided its members with a modest financial return, covered some lending losses (bad debts) and put aside the amount 'left over' into a lending loss reserve. The Directors have set a target for the lending loss reserve of 5% of lending capacity and barring any unforeseen losses in the next few weeks, we should reach that target at the end of this financial year.

So, we might generate some 'surplus' for the first time this year, after we have paid interest to members and met our lending loss reserve target. We cannot rely on generating a surplus in any given year as it may be affected by our performance, unforeseen costs or lending losses. Therefore anything we choose to do with these surpluses must be on the basis that we can only commit funds after we are sure of the final year end position.

The Society's rules are very specific and only allow us to apply net profits to: pay interest to members; set aside reserve funds (such as our lending loss reserve) to meet any contingency affecting the business of the Society; pay a rebate on the charges made by the Society by persons other than members (i.e. interest charged to our borrowers); set aside an education fund for the purpose of promoting education relating to the Objects of the Society; set aside money to a common fund to be used for charitable purposes; simply carry forward any profits not set aside as above.

The article expanded on each of these options and invited the members to write in with their views. In the end paying a rebate to producers met with general approval and it was further agreed to pay the rebate in priority to members' interest.

Three years after Stephanie had taken on the role of Managing Director, Shared Interest had progressed enormously. The lending portfolio had expanded significantly and for the first time in its history Shared Interest was celebrating having made a surplus. But ahead loomed the difficulty of low interest rates and with an increased portfolio, the difficulty of how to offer finance to the whole of the fair trade movement when it was imperative for Shared Interest to have prudential limits in place in order to protect its portfolio.

INTERCRAFTS

Intercrafts Peru is a part of CIAP (Central Interegional Peruvian Artisans). It exports products created by 700 artisans spread throughout the whole of Peru to customers in all parts of the world

CHAPTER 7
COMMODITY RISK

"More than 20 million people throughout the world are connected to the coffee production cycle and rely on the crop as their primary income source. Fair trade has emerged as a powerful tool to support many of those farmers and workers build pathways out of poverty. Shared Interest played a pioneering role creating trade credit mechanisms enabling those farmer organizations to finance their dreams."
Jonathan Rosenthal, Consultant to Shared Interest

W hen the concept of the Clearing House was being developed in the mid to late 1990s, the obvious strategic partner at the time was the International Federation for Alternative Trade (IFAT). Access to Shared Interest's financial services was only available through membership of IFAT, thus saving Shared Interest from making any independent assessment of an organisation's fair trade credentials. This worked very well in the main as the majority of the fair trade buyer organisations were members of IFAT and many of the fair trade handicraft producers also developed a network for themselves through membership of IFAT.

The gap though was in the area of commodities such as coffee, tea and cocoa. Commodity producers had little in common with handicraft producers and therefore very few were members of IFAT. Some producers during the 1990s had been able to gain the support of Shared Interest as they sold to fair trade buyers who were members of IFAT but for the most part, they were unable to access direct finance from Shared Interest.

For Shared Interest, this untapped market was inaccessible anyway as the commodity limits that they had put in place in 1994 meant there wasn't any spare finance available to lend to the likes of coffee producers in Latin America. It was already at full capacity by lending to the fair trade coffee buyers such as Equal Exchange Inc.

In the summer 1997 edition of Quarterly Return, Shared Interest reported on the issues that are caused as the 'Coffee Price Soars':

You may have noticed that there has been an increase in the price of coffee in the shops.

This reflects a recent shortage of coffee due to a number of reasons. These range from an uncertainty in the supply from crucial Arabica producers in Colombia and Brazil, where rumours of frost and industrial disputes have been a problem, to poor weather during the harvesting period. As a result, the price of coffee has doubled.

Ironically, while a rise in the price of coffee may be good for farmers, it is not necessarily good for fair trade. Commercial buyers side-line the fair trade organisations and reap the benefits of the high prices. In the long run this is not good for the farmers, as the commercial buyers feel no commitment to them when the market is not so lucrative.

Coffee is a notoriously volatile product and the price fluctuates dramatically. One of the ways in which the fair trade buyers, such as Equal Exchange Inc in America and Gepa in Germany, help to protect the farmers against the volatility, is to offer a fair trade minimum price. Obviously when the market price is below this, the producer organisations can keep the loyalty of the individual farmers. The problems arise when the price rockets and the local traders (sometimes called coyotes because of their predatory nature) move in offering immediate cash.

When this happens the producer organisations or secondary cooperatives based in the countries are the ones who suffer; when they come to buy the coffee they find there is very little left. Some of these farmers perhaps only produce one bag of coffee and cannot resist the coyote's offer, even though they know that when the price comes down again, as it inevitably does, the coyotes will abandon them.

Because the fair trade movement does not have huge reserves of cash and cannot speculate on the price of coffee, they are unable to find the extra cash immediately when the price of coffee goes up, although in the long run they will pay the farmers better than the commercial rate. And so the producer coops who have taken orders from fair trade buyers months before, and have even paid advances to the farmers, find themselves unable to fulfil these orders and can quickly get into trouble. This can only be bad news for the farmers.

Shared Interest has stepped in to help overcome the crisis, by increasing credit facilities to enable both buyers and producer organisations to fund the increased costs of coffee beans. However to protect our investors the Board has decided that no more than 15% of share capital should be directly exposed to the risk involved in the coffee market.

While this 'crisis' brought about a temporary increased prudential limit of 15% of share capital meaning that more producers could access finance, it was clear that there were many more who desperately needed access. Shared Interest continued to consider how it could work with more coffee producers without taking on excessive risk.

Before he finally left the Board of Shared Interest, in the summer of 2001 Mark Hayes presented to the Board a theory of hedging – as a way of managing price fluctuations – in commodity markets. If the price fluctuation risk could be managed satisfactorily it might be possible for Shared Interest to increase its commodity limit and lend more to coffee producers. Though, as Mark explained, this idea would come at a cost. He explained the need for more research and the cost of carrying out that research. The first requirement would be to research among producers and buyers to see if there was sufficient demand to justify the cost of the steps needed to bring a study to completion. If there was sufficient interest, Mark proposed that the research and pilot study could be completed by December 2002.

At the March 2002 board meeting, Jonathan Rosenthal, who had been working with fair trade coffee for 20 years with Equal Exchange Inc and then as an independent consultant joined the meeting and made a presentation on his work on this project. There were essentially two parts to his presentation, the first was a discussion of technical points about the project and the second, the next steps for the Society in the light of progress made to date.

The technical discussion was mainly about the performance risk if the project came to fruition. Solving the problem of commodity price fluctuation for the fair trade market was a vital piece of the jigsaw that was missing. Even the World Bank had a project underway but was stumbling over performance risk (the general risk of non-delivery rather than specific price-fluctuation risk). The defining feature of the Society's proposal was that the Society was prepared to assume the performance risk, passing it on to members as a last resort. The performance risk on any contract might last from two to six months. Jonathan did though point out that, during his research he had spoken to some derivatives traders with experience in the area who did not think the proposed hedging scheme could work. Their issue was that the practical difficulties of making bargains could lead to timing problems that could be very expensive. Human error or technological failure could be disproportionately risky if large positions were left open. During turbulent market conditions it might be impossible to make the deals needed, for instance if no one else was willing to make a bargain.

The discussion then turned to the best way forward for the Society. There was a consensus that the work should proceed as far as preparing a pilot study for discussion at the strategy meeting in July 2002. It was clear that any solution emanating from the pilot study needed to handle the risk from a 'southern' as well as a 'northern' perspective. This was at the same time recognising that producers seem to want to manage their own risk. Presenting a 'northern' solution to 'southern' risk might create antagonism.

The day after this board meeting, was the Annual General Meeting of Shared Interest which was addressed by Harriet Lamb, Executive Director of the Fairtrade Foundation. Tracy Bonham, then a Voluntary Rep and later a staff member, recalls: *"Harriet Lamb speaking at the AGM was a turning point for me. She was an inspirational speaker."*

Quarterly Return in the Spring of 2002 reported on Harriet's speech in a piece entitled 'Passion, practicality and determination':

"We are witnessing the start of a quiet revolution in shopping and investment," said Harriet Lamb, as she announced that sales of Fairtrade marked products in the UK had grown by over 40% in the last year.

The Fairtrade Foundation is the UK member of an international alliance – FLO – of 17 organisations which are working together to monitor universally recognised standards in Fairtrade. Eight commodities – coffee, tea, sugar, honey, cocoa/chocolate, bananas, mangoes and orange juice – are currently eligible for the Fairtrade mark and other fruits, rice and cotton will soon be included.

"Fairtrade is an enormous challenge," said Harriet Lamb. "We expect small, disadvantaged farmers to compete head-to-head with multinational companies. And we ask more of them. Not only high-quality produce, but also Fairtrade production conditions.

We also expect a lot from buyers of Fairtrade products. They must accept terms of trade that their commercial competitors would refuse to accept, and still make a profit."

As Jonathan Rosenthal began work on the pilot study, he soon felt that the Society's scheme could not work in isolation and the best route forward would be to become part of the World Bank's initiative. He knew that the interface with the World Bank would be difficult and expensive to manage but might have the advantage of bringing the Society's work with farmers more into the mainstream.

As part of the pilot study, Jonathan had engaged with an independent commodity trading consultant, David Waite and it was clear from David's report that the key problem seemed to be that producers themselves did not find the scheme sufficiently attractive.

With these two points in mind, Jonathan was asked to stop working on the pilot scheme and instead investigate the costs of the Society's proposed scheme challenging David Waite's view about whether the unique nature of the share capital the Society has available and the lower financial returns the Society's shareholders were seeking made the proposal more likely to succeed. It was agreed it would be worthwhile keeping in touch with the World Bank's team and Philip Angier in his capacity as a Board Director was asked to attend the next meeting of the World Bank International Task Force (ITF) on Risk Management in Abidjan, Côte d'Ivoire in June 2002.

In Philip's report to the Board he said that the World Bank's International Task Force project was focused on small farmers, not 'Fairtrade' and therefore might not in the long run enable the Society to lend more using their present criteria. Both Philip's report and the latest report from Jonathan Rosenthal, recommended Shared Interest became involved with the ITF in order to learn more about commodity price risk management. It would also allow them to become involved in appropriate networks and get access to (otherwise expensive) expertise in the field. It would also allow them to gain a wide range of producer perspectives and take part in some pilots.

On the other side of the coin, involvement with the ITF might also give Shared Interest the possibility of opening up Fairtrade ideas to the World Bank and the commodity market generally and also might allow Shared Interest to act as interlocutor between marginalised producer cooperatives and market institutions.

With this option of working with the ITF opening up, there was also speculation about whether the Society could raise funds (a *"coffee pot"*) for a risky venture into the Fairtrade coffee market separate from the existing share capital. A fund of £5-£10m might be needed for an initial foray. The idea of lending further, riskier, funds in coffee might however run in tandem with the ITF project and would give Shared Interest the advantage of being able to actually enter the market with some loan funds, alongside the risk management activity. It was agreed that the Society should pursue the ITF project as long as it would reach the Fairtrade producers the Society was concerned about and it was agreed that attempts should be made to have the Society's involvement part-funded by the ITF and/or others. It was understood that theoretically the ITF scheme reduced performance risk during a price spike because of the availability of both hedging contracts and credit to small producers but understanding these risks would need work.

In Quarterly Return Issue 45 in the autumn of 2002, Jonathan Rosenthal explained to members why coffee is the commodity that causes the most concern and greatest hope for fair trade campaigners:

People are often perplexed and question why coffee has such a dominant role in fair trade. A staple of nearly every household in the industrialised world, it is one of the globe's most heavily traded legal commodities, second only to oil as a source of foreign exchange for Third World countries.

Coffee is an ideal product for fair trade because its product life cycle provides a stark illustration of the inequities of world markets and the relationships between struggling farmers and consumers in rich countries.

Coffee has deep roots in the Developing World. The crop covers almost half of the permanently farmed land in the neotropics and tropics of Latin America and the Caribbean, which together produce two thirds of the world's coffee.

Small coffee farmers are well organised compared to other commodity growers, and their products cannot be grown in the consuming countries. More than 20 million people throughout the world are connected to the coffee production cycle and rely on the crop as their primary income source.

There are also many marketing reasons for coffee's leading role in fair trade.

It is fairly expensive and relatively non-perishable, making it an attractive product for small retailers and large-scale operations alike. Its compact packaging makes the product easily transportable. At the same time, roasting and packaging can be done in the consuming country. This makes it a less risky proposition for fair trade marketers than some other products that are fully processed at the producing end. Unfortunately, this advantage keeps more of the wealth generated from seed to cup in the consuming country, a distinct drawback for farmers.

In the same newsletter Stephanie explained Shared Interest's coffee policy:

Financing fair trade is both an opportunity and a threat for Shared Interest.

Fair trade provides farmers with some stability, certainty and a decent income. The fair trade price is currently set at $1.26/lb for green beans, compared with a world market price below $0.60/lb and a 'farm gate' price much lower still. The fair trade price has been above the market price for a few years and it has therefore been effectively a fixed price – easy to administer and finance.

Usually the world market price is reasonably stable, subject to small fluctuations with trends moving up and down gradually. But occasionally – about every seven years – the world market price rises very rapidly to three or four times its normal level. Such volatility is a serious problem for farmers and also for lenders.

The main risk to fair trade buyers and Shared Interest is that smallholder farmers will not deliver. Contracts for delivery of coffee are normally struck months in advance with secondary coffee cooperatives at an agreed price. In a price spike, individual farmers are persuaded to sell their beans 'off the bush' to private traders, rather than delivering, as agreed to their primary cooperative. The primary cooperative usually does not have sufficient credit to pay the inflated local market price in cash to those farmers who can deliver. This in turn leads to default on delivery to secondary cooperatives and ultimately in turn to fair trade buyers. Because we provide credit against confirmed orders, if there is no delivery, we cannot be repaid and the producer will default. There may also be sudden increases in the demand for both producer and buyer credit to pay the increased prices.

A less immediate risk is the possibility of future losses by fair trade buyers if they cannot pass on the high price to the consumer, particularly if they are left holding large quantities of expensive stock.

For many years we have recognized the need to control the risk to Shared Interest by limiting our exposure to coffee to 10% of share capital. Even at the 10% limit, a sudden price rise could potentially use up most of our liquid funds. Any more than 10% and in the event of a default by borrowers, our very existence may be threatened.

The problem seems far away with world coffee prices depressed for a long time and farmers going out of business. However, it is a real issue that cannot be ignored and will come back at some point in the future.

This issue has vexed us for a long time. It is clear we could lend far more in fair trade coffee if only we could reduce the risks associated with price volatility. We have already looked at a possible hedging system that involves Shared Interest intervening to buy and sell futures contracts to create price insurance for farmers and traders. However, this appeared to be too costly and represents a 'northern solution' to a 'southern problem'. We have also started to take a look at the valuable work done with farmers by the World Bank International Task Force (ITF) for commodity risk management. Working with the ITF might present us with some real possibilities for engaging with farmers to try out some risk management tools – we shall be exploring this further.

By January 2003 a progress report emanating from the work with the ITF signalled that the project would develop more slowly than had been expected. This cast doubt on both the timing of and the need for the recruitment of a member of staff to support the project.

By this time, the World Bank's International Task Force (ITF) had already successfully trained some small producers and intermediaries in the use of financial instruments to spread risk and use the markets to provide a measure of price protection. While price insurance creates liquidity in the market it does not remove all the risk in the transaction. In particular, the performance risk remained although, arguably, it was reduced if producers had more robust finances.

With work with the ITF ongoing, the staff at Shared Interest were starting to have contact with many different FLO producers aside from coffee producers. This early contact had identified some preliminary issues to consider before any credit could be offered to FLO producers. In particular many FLO producers often deal with only one buyer which made it impossible for them to provide three buyer references in the way that IFAT producers gain access to the Society's credit. It was therefore agreed to accept any three references for FLO producers at least one of which must be a buyer. It was also noted that these food producers in contrast to the handicraft producers, were much bigger organisations and the requests were for large facilities, often more than 1% of share capital. This meant each would have to be considered on a case by case basis.

While some FLO registered producers sold to Fairtrade buyers, many sold directly to commercial buyers and it was against these orders primarily that they were looking for credit. Historically, Shared Interest had only offered credit against commercial orders to IFAT producers they had worked with for a year, providing them with credit against their orders to fair trade buyers during the course of that initial year. It was agreed as this policy wasn't helpful for FLO producers working with commercial buyers that they would be able to access credit against commercial orders without any qualifying period, again though on a case by case basis.

The Clearing House at the time was branded jointly by IFAT and the Society and it was discussed internally how adding FLO to the branding for the work with their producers was an attractive idea. It was recognised however that there were problems with this idea because FLO is an accreditation organisation rather than a membership based organisation and the lack of availability of funds to offer coffee producers (the largest group within the FLO registers) was a major obstacle to making any proposition to FLO.

Early in 2003, it was proposed to concentrate further research on finding ways to strengthen the Society's capacity to accommodate the risks in coffee rather than mechanisms to transfer the risk elsewhere. This would mean developing 'balance sheet' options rather than technical solutions to price risk. It was agreed that Shared Interest should maintain links with the World

Bank's International Task Force and others and be a minority partner in any emerging alliance of organisations working in the field as this was clearly important to developing the knowledge of the Society.

Indeed by the middle of 2003, it was proposed to remove the coffee commodity limit of 10% of share capital as the 10% limit was already substantially breached and a new method of managing the risks was needed. Instead the proposed risk management system did not propose an overall limit on coffee so theoretically coffee lending, subject to suitable risk management procedures, could reach 100% of share capital. The Board however decided to retain the fixed coffee limit during the initial implementation of the risk management procedures while recognizing that if at some point in the future the *"Coffee Pot"* idea was to go ahead then up to 50% of the loan portfolio could end up being in coffee. But without such a pot, coffee loans would probably level out at about 30% of the portfolio if the risk management system's suggestions were acceptable.

It was recognized that all of this could only really be pulled together by a dedicated resource and so in 2004, Roy Parizat was appointed as Project Leader to work on this project.

In Spring 2006 in an article by Shared Interest's Account Manager for Latin America, Will Cowell, Quarterly Return reported on the next stage:

In 2004 Shared Interest appointed Roy Parizat to lead its 'commodities project' and investigate how we could safely increase the amount of our members' investment we could use for coffee lending. In November last year Roy and I travelled to Latin America to road-test his proposals, learn more about the coffee industry and see for ourselves the social impact of our lending.

Roy had devised a coffee 'scorecard' addressing the main risk areas of a coffee cooperative and determining the level of risk involved in lending to it. The success criteria for the scorecard was to go and use it and see if it worked on some potential new lending for Shared Interest. We visited coffee cooperatives in Costa Rica, Peru and Mexico and I am pleased to say that the trip is promising to be a resounding success.

The scorecard proved itself to be an effective tool and we returned with several new lending opportunities.

When Roy's work went to the Board, his recommendation was to increase the commodity limit risk to 30% but it was agreed that the current working limit should be 20%, subject to a Board review when that limit was reached.

A year later QR reported on the Speciality Coffee Association of America (SCAA) conference that staff attended in May 2007:

"Meetings with fair trade coffee producers from across Latin America raised the prospect of new business totalling $600,000 in term loans and $2.3m in pre-finance."

Commercial Manager Ben Lilley said: *"It was a highly successful trip which proved just how much awareness there is among commodities producers for the benefits that Shared Interest can bring to their businesses."*

Even in 2010, the unsatisfied demand for finance from coffee producers is high. Shared Interest continues to limit its coffee exposure to 35% of share capital with an additional regional limit in place. A risk profile is maintained on each coffee customer with a view to taking specific actions depending on the customer's risk profile. The new prudential limit allows Shared Interest to progress proposals and increase the Society's lending income, while controlling the regional risks associated with coffee lending.

KAYONZA

Kayonza Tea Growers' Factory is located in
South West Uganda and was established in 1963.
It has over 5,000 smallholder tea growers and
they have been partners with Cafédirect since
1998. 14% of the growers are women

CHAPTER 8
DELIVERING
THE VISION

"These investors of Shared Interest are doing a noble thing. Their money is reaching people who are prepared to work, people who really need it and are seen as unbankable by the commercial banks. They have no access to cash, not much information and not much opportunity. To know help is at hand from Shared Interest gives power to the poor."
Pauline Ntombura, Managing Director, Salom

———◆———

S tephanie's first three years in office had been focused on the takeover of Bridgehead and establishing and significantly increasing lending through the Clearing House. The work on commodities and how to lend more to certified food producers was ongoing but a lot was still to come in the second half of Stephanie's seven-year term as Managing Director.

In her budget back in 2001/02 Stephanie had proposed paying for the first time a 0% interest to members in order to produce a forecast with the target 1% profit level. It was assumed in this budget that lending activities would continue to develop at the present rate. By this time a range of fair trade organisations were working with Shared Interest, as was reflected in one edition of Quarterly Return, Issue 46. In a piece written by Leslie Rowe, Finance Director, he described 'Fair trade down under':

Go into any of the 17 Oxfam Trading shops in the major urban areas of Australia and you will be greeted with an Aladdin's cave of goods from different communities around the world. Unlike shops in the UK, Oxfam Australia Trading does not sell second hand goods. These shops are very up-market.

Oxfam Australia Trading has brought Fair Trade to the shopping malls of Australia. The partnership with Shared Interest allows Oxfam Australia Trading to engage actively in supporting producers, awareness raising and in campaigning for changes in the rules and practices of international trade.

In the same edition of Quarterly Return Allison Barrett, Producer Liaison Officer, reported on one of the Clearing House's newest members, Lombok Pottery Centre in Indonesia:

In the village of Babamanyuk the signs of pottery are everywhere; women shaping large bowls on their verandahs, a young girl walking with a basket of pots balanced on her head, dry clay spread out on the road, being crushed to powder with the help of passers-by walking or cycling over it. There is no room for cars in the lanes between the thatched houses.

Just 15 years ago, Babamanyuk, which is on the Indonesian Island of Lombok, was very poor; the houses were makeshift and the children did not go to school. A New Zealand potter, Jean McKinnon, came to the village and thought that with a little help, these people could find a market for their traditional pottery. She managed to persuade the New Zealand government to fund a project, the Lombok Pottery Centre, which for seven years worked with the villagers, helping them with new equipment and training to develop their crude pots into marketable items. Just two years after they began selling their ceramics, the Centre became self sufficient, and now as the demand for Lombok pottery has grown, some of their potters too have become independent and have opened their own shops.

Early in 2002, ideas for expanding the lending opportunities through the Clearing House were being considered. One such proposal was to lend to members of the British Association for Fair Trade Shops. Although some felt the focus should be maintained on direct lending to Third World producers and it was difficult to forget that the Society's first bad debt had been to a fair trade retailer, it was felt overall that the scheme proposed might provide a welcome boost to the European retail fair trade sector and so it was approved.

At the annual strategy meeting in the summer of 2002 Sue Mayo, Business Development Manager presented a paper which analysed the current fair trade market and proposed a lending budget based on a detailed business development plan. The discussion following the presentation concentrated on the need to develop existing contacts in IFAT and expand the Society's work into new areas of the fair trade market. It was noted that while steady growth was anticipated, the rate of growth would not be as strong as that in the last three years as there were now only a limited number of IFAT buyers that Shared Interest did not already work with. The focus instead was to look at the many possibilities of working with more IFAT producers, but with new producer facilities being relatively small this would have limited impact on the total portfolio. Increasing the membership base of IFAT was one helpful way to increase the potential for lending to Shared Interest and it was with this in mind that Shared Interest had agreed a three year sponsorship of a new post, the IFAT Membership Officer. Hilary Thorndike was appointed into this post and recalls this time:

"Shared Interest funded my position from 2001-2004. My role was extremely diverse, following up with the backlog of WFTO (formerly known as IFAT) registering new members. This wouldn't have been done without funding from Shared Interest so I am extremely grateful to them.

"The IFAT logo was launched in 2002-2003 which gave a new dimension to my role. Being an IFAT member opened up many doors for producers and one of the most significant was Shared Interest, enabling producers to access fair finance was a massive step forward and one which the producers placed a high value on and greatly appreciated as it was not offered to them from anywhere else.

"Part of my role was to spread the word about Shared Interest and fair finance and I felt extremely proud to be doing this as I knew the impact it would make on the businesses we were working with. The producers had to be members of IFAT for at least a year before being able to access fair finance through Shared Interest, showing their dedication to the fair trade movement.

"The response from producers about Shared Interest was always positive. It is a very clear system that works. The visual aid of the triangle (Clearing House system) always worked extremely well, especially when working with producers whose literacy rates were sometimes low and across language barriers.

"The producers were excited by the concept of Shared Interest as it provided them with support (in terms of capital up front and loans) which they greatly valued and which enabled many of them to take their business to the next level.

"I greatly admired producers who took the leap into the fair trade world. For many of them this leap was no mean feat, they had to produce annual accounts, and change the way they managed their business. It took a lot of time and energy with no returns guaranteed.

"I'm very grateful to Shared Interest for giving me this opportunity. I absolutely loved my role, especially the diversity of it. In one day I would email in French and then pick up the phone and have a conversation in Portuguese. There are not many jobs in which you get to speak to people from all over the globe – luckily for me I am a linguist!"

While Shared Interest was looking to the future, it also had a new situation to consider in the present. For the first time in the history of Shared Interest, the Society was predicted to have committed more than its trade lending capacity before the end of 2003. At the time lending capacity was fixed at 80% of share capital and therefore the cumulative committed facilities agreed with fair trade organisations had for the first time in its history exceeded this 80% of share capital or trade lending capacity, as it was known. While the size of each individual committed facility was fixed, inevitably the amount drawn down on this facility was rarely at 100% for the entire duration of a year. With this in mind, it was proposed to change the way of considering the overall portfolio – clearly the amount drawn at any one time was the more critical amount and so it was set that drawn lending should not exceed 75% of lending capacity. It was agreed that commitments could be increased until drawn lending approached this limit at which point it would need to be reviewed again.

At the same time, it was noted that profitability was being squeezed by lower UK interest rates and the few Social Banks that Shared Interest deposited its money with were also paying low rates of interest. As a consequence it was agreed that the liquidity target of 20% of share capital should remain but that it would no longer be necessary to strive to keep the whole of the 20% invested in Social Banks. (The rest of cash was kept with UK ethical banks (like the Co-op) and UK mutual building societies).

It was noted within the budget for 2003 that costs were projected to rise faster than income and there was a debate about the level of operating costs. There were no direct comparators but larger co-operatives, banks and building societies at the time had lower costs as a percentage of share capital, but some thought that similar size social finance businesses tended to have higher cost ratios than the Society. It was noted that the ability of the Society both to pay an interest rate to members and to offer customers loans at reasonable interest rates was partly dependent upon being able to contain operating and development costs.

With drawn lending increasing, it was recognised that there would soon be a need to substantially increase share capital. With this in mind, the results of the membership survey actioned in 2001, were studied to gain a valuable insight into how best to increase share capital. The findings from the membership survey had been reported in Quarterly Return in the autumn of 2001:

A questionnaire was posted to all 8,448 members and we received a superb 61% response from 5,158 members. This, in itself, says something about our membership. They are extremely interested, active and keen to contribute.

Our membership is 57% female and older than the general population – 41% of members are retired, compared with 26% of the general population. Younger people are extremely under-represented and, as a result, our members have far fewer children living at home than the general population. Those who are employed tend to work in health, education or government – 57% compared with 25% in the general population. Our members are extremely well qualified with virtually no-one without a qualification; 60% have a first degree; 25% have a higher degree and 58% have a professional qualification. Our members are predominantly white – 99% compared with 94% of the general population.

Our members have other ethical investments – 38% with the Co-op, 31% have a Triodos account, 24% have an ethical fund investment.

By far the most popular national newspaper among members is the Guardian (35%), followed by its sister paper the Observer (15%). The most popular magazine is the New Internationalist (12%).

Three-quarters of our members are Christians, mostly 'active'. Other religions are not well represented – only 2% compared with 14% of the population. Our members are active fair trade consumers – 60% buy fairly traded goods regularly, with 39% buying occasionally.

Most of our members (83%) have less than 10% of their savings with us, 88% of members see their investment as 'lower risk', 87% thought the level of risk we take was 'about right' and only 12% thought we should take more risk.

Overall 93% of members were satisfied or extremely satisfied with the way Shared Interest uses their money.

At the September 2002 board meeting Stephanie presented a further analysis of the 2001 membership survey data, carried out by the University of Northumbria:

- The regional analysis and the age profiles were highlighted
    - Younger and more sceptical members were located in London.
    - Older more religious members were located in Scotland.
    - Older members liked QR better.
    - Internet use was at 90% among the under 35s.
- Support for development charities was strong and higher than previously reported (due to an error in the initial analysis the previous year).
- The survey appeared to confirm the anecdotal evidence that the development-aware section of society was the most fruitful for membership recruitment.
- Membership was skewed in favour of the south of the UK and so it was felt it might be wise to hold the 'third' or 'no fixed abode' AGM in the three year cycle in the South, maybe in the Bristol area.

Early in 2003, Stephanie presented a paper for a project that was to be called 'Delivering the Vision' and the focus of the project was on getting closer to producers and gaining better information about their organisations, products, local contexts and credit needs. For Shared Interest it was proposed to have more of a presence *"in the field"* working with local partners and agencies to bring much needed credit to more trading organisations. The idea was to establish an overseas *"sales force"* largely from local people and agencies that understood the languages, customs and markets of their region. This idea was developed by the management team.

It was noted to the Board that building an international sales force would present Shared Interest with some tough challenges – to the organisational structure, to the technology and communications systems and to all the people involved. The change could not be undertaken rapidly and the development would have to be phased.

The first phase Stephanie proposed was to focus on the organisational review. There would be some substantial change. For example business development would overlap with the operational areas of the business. Once the detail of the organisational review had been shared with the Board, it was recognised that Stephanie would have to devote a lot of time and energy to the change process.

The next phase would then be the delivery of improved customer services and building an international network with the long-term objective of establishing an international presence (see chapter 9). Internally work therefore began on preparing the organisation for its next era – an organisation with an international presence.

Externally, 2003 was a significant year for Shared Interest as it jointly hosted with Traidcraft, IFAT's 7th biennial conference, 'Speaking out for Fair Trade'. The conference was held from 22-28th June at Newcastle University and over the weekend of 21st and 22nd June, 250 people from more than 50 countries in Africa, Asia, Latin America, Europe, North America and Pacific Rim arrived in Newcastle upon Tyne.

The conference theme 'Speaking out for Fair Trade' allowed delegates to talk about how they communicated to a wider, global audience about the unique proposition of fair trade. It enabled delegates to discuss the ongoing need to campaign to the world stage, the demands that they needed to meet and the monitoring they carried out to build trust in fair trade, giving them the confidence to speak out. For many delegates, it was the most outward facing conference in the history of IFAT.

Quarterly Return, Issue 48, Summer 2003 reported on the opening forum and quoted from the speeches of the main speakers:

The opening forum was both self congratulatory and challenging.

First to speak was Francisco VanderHoff Boersma, founder of UCIRI Mexico and co-founder of Max Havelaar, Netherlands: *"It is not enough to protest. We must also propose,"* he said. *"If we want to challenge the unfair structures of international trade we must propose an alternative system."*

Terry Hudghton, Head of Corporate Brand Management at the Co-operative Group explained why the Co-op has put so much effort into fair trade. *"There are two reasons why the Co-op has put so much into fair trade"* he said. *"Firstly, we are a consumer-owned business and fair trade is a growing consumer issue. And secondly the aims of fair trade are complementary to the cooperative values and principles."*

The next speaker, Dr Alan Knight OBE, Head of Social Responsibility at the Kingfisher Group, said he felt as though he was stepping into the lions' den by agreeing to speak at this forum. *"Our corporate strategy is built around globalisation"* he admitted. *"But this global buying power has helped Kingfisher to implement some particularly enlightening sourcing policies. For example, all timber and wood products stocked by B&Q come from sustainable sources certified by the Forestry Stewardship Council. We didn't do this out of idealism,"* he said, *"we did it because we feared that bad publicity would affect our business."*

The conference reached out to a much broader audience than ever before, providing delegates, especially those from producer organisations, with many new contacts. Open days on 22nd June and 28th June drew visitors from the business world, government, local community and donor organisations as well as fair trade supporters including Shared Interest members.

One of Shared Interest's voluntary Representatives, Elsie Fairbanks commented: *"Following my time at the IFAT conference in June, I feel even more convinced that Shared Interest has a vital and irreplaceable role to play in the whole process of fair trade. Hearing real stories about the bureaucracy and the length of time that producer groups have been faced with when trying to obtain loans, and the high interest rates demanded, versus the speed and simplicity of the Shared Interest process is a testament in itself."*

The main conference focused on market development, the promotion of fair trade, fair trade monitoring, and the overall strategic direction for the fair trade movement represented in IFAT. Each day began with a personal testimony on fair trade, each a poignant reminder of the hopes of vulnerable people engaged in small scale enterprise everywhere.

Members used the space provided at the University throughout the conference to exhibit their products and conduct meetings with buyers. 90 producer members took advantage of the opportunity and 40 external buyers accepted invitations to meet them in addition to the buyer members of IFAT. The IFAT members have always felt that this 'marketplace' was a very important part of each IFAT conference.

On the final day, two thirds of the conference delegates took part in a Trade Justice Campaign rally in Newcastle City Centre.

With the IFAT conference behind them, it was time for Shared Interest to return to internal matters. In November 2003 the Board returned to the subject of producer rebates which had been discussed in Quarterly Return in the autumn of 2001 (see chapter 6). It was recognised that the subject of rebates had become very complicated and in the end it was proposed that there should be no rebate in 2002/2003. This was justified under the present system as Shared Interest had made a significant provision for a bad debt for a producer loan.

In the winter of 2003/2004, Shared Interest published its 50th edition of

Quarterly Return, with all three editors taking a turn at reflecting on the way the newsletter to the members had changed:

Keith Richardson, editor 1992-1995 commented: *"what I want to briefly touch on here are not the headlines but, for me, more important events.*

"The first event was very personal. It was a simple realization that came from research I conducted with members and from feedback to QR. This found that many of our members felt that they had enough money for their needs and could use what they had spare to invest in Shared Interest. It struck me at the time as an amazing concept in an age of rampant consumerism that people could say this and act on it.

"We successfully show that profit and social purpose are not incompatible and, as part of a growing movement of social enterprises that make a profit for a social purpose, we can make a real impact on the world."

Allison Barrett, editor 1995-2002 commented: *"Reading back through the issues that I edited reminds me how much Shared Interest has grown and changed since I joined as Promotion Officer in 1995. At that time, there were just two and a half members of staff, now there are nearly 20.*

"After 27 issues of QR I feel my greatest reward has been the privilege of getting to know the producers and bringing their inspiring stories to you through these pages."

David Parker, editor 2002-current day commented: *"For me the most memorable event over the last two years was the hosting of the IFAT biennial conference in Newcastle upon Tyne. This gave our members a unique opportunity to meet many producers, who seemed equally keen to meet their overseas investors."*

With the focus on looking forward and expanding its lending by setting up an international presence, Shared Interest acknowledged that perhaps the time had come to do some serious analysis of the social impact it was having. Even back as early as 1996 Shared Interest had been considering the possibility of social reporting alongside its financial reporting. In a meeting in 1996 the work of Traidcraft in this field was noted. It was felt at the time that much of the review of business that Shared Interest published annually concentrated on its effectiveness in reaching producers. At the time it was also noted that social reporting was still in its infancy and that different organisations had different approaches to the reports.

The topic was returned to in May 1999 when Stephanie introduced a paper on social audit. She proposed a staged approach to the audit beginning with a thorough consideration of the principles of audit. She emphasised that she did not want to lock into a process that was not useful to the Society.

In July 2002 a more concerted effort was made to measure the Society's impact on poverty. Colin Crawford presented on progress with the 'Defining our Role in Fair Trade' (DRIFT) project. He explained that producer and buyer interviews had been conducted mostly at IFAT regional meetings and an initial survey of impact studies in fair trade had been carried out. It was recognised that there were some difficulties in making sure meaningful responses to questionnaires were received as interviews for the project were carried out by Shared Interest staff.

At the time though it was recognised that this was not a social accounting project but a *"scoping exercise"* to help Shared Interest define what they might want to measure in the future. There was some concern that the project could not achieve many meaningful results because it was aimed at defining Shared Interest's impact in 'fair trade' (an indirect measure) rather than its direct impact in 'poverty alleviation'. (This was not a unique problem – it was common to all 'secondary' or 'support' organisations, particularly in the cooperative movement).

At the September 2002 meeting, Stephanie presented an interim report on the results of the customer questionnaires/interviews, which concluded that some measures of the Society's social impact could be developed as a result of the DRIFT exercise. The information from the questionnaires was wide-ranging and exceedingly useful. Buyers made points about the need for alternative funding for a variety of business uses and were forthright that availability of credit increased the amount of purchases from producers. The information about producers' alternative sources of credit and the costs of these was also particularly interesting. It was also interesting to note how Shared Interest's customers saw them – with few producers seeing the Society as closely associated with IFAT (whereas most buyers made this association).

An incremental approach to social reporting was recommended, rather than a sudden expensive exercise. It was recognised that information needed to be obtained independently and externally verified.

In May 2003 Stephanie circulated a paper and explained the background to the attempts that had been made to introduce social reporting. It had foundered on the lack of a clear statement about the Society's mission and overall aims. Social reporting needed key indicators of achievement to operate. As a result of this the mission statement was reviewed. Both Board and Council had done some work on revising it and at the AGM in 2003, members had been presented with a number of draft mission statements on which they had been invited to give their comments. What came out clearly was that within the mission stakeholders felt there needed to be a focus on poverty alleviation and partnership between North and South. Also felt to be important were justice, trade and financial services. In the end it took 18 months to agree a mission statement that all stakeholders were satisfied with.

The paper presented to the May 2003 board meeting included a report of the survey work undertaken among the Society's customers, the draft mission statement, a summary of published work on the effect of fair trade and proposals for key indicators to be developed from existing information sources in a fully costed programme.

This information formed the groundwork for the social reporting process which was then finally initiated in May 2005. It was noted that during the first year of social reporting, it is the process and knowledge gained that is more important than the finished publication. The process and knowledge gained then act as the benchmark for future years. It was also noted that further understanding of the social impact of lending could help to make decisions about new lending in the future.

In December 2005 the project team, after a steep learning curve to prepare their first set of social accounts, were congratulated on producing a quality document, attracting high praise from the audit panel. The process of producing the social accounts was explained to the Board at a meeting early in 2006 and the necessity of using a project team and existing data wherever possible was emphasised.

It was recognised that the social accounts contained a wealth of information, but that the format and length would probably prove a barrier to many readers. It was agreed that the social accounts should be specifically edited for transparency and publication on the web and it was also recommended that general guidance notes for readers of the social accounts should be provided. It was further agreed that there would be an executive summary for each section of the social accounts with links to each section, which would be downloadable in PDF format. Hard copies would be provided only on request.

During the years since then Shared Interest has won several awards for its social accounts. These include commendation in the ACCA Awards for

Sustainability Reporting 2006 for Best First Time Reporter, for their 2004/5 social accounts. Shared Interest's 2005/6 social accounts were commended in the SME category of the ACCA awards 2007. Shared Interest also received a runners up award in the UK smaller organisations category of the CIPFA/PriceWaterhouseCooper Public Reporting and Accountability Awards. They received a Judges Special Award for successfully incorporating their social accounting into their overall reporting strategy and lastly, also in 2007 they were a finalist for a Third Sector Excellent Award for Governance and Transparency.

Towards the end of 2005, the Society moved into a new era again when Stephanie Sturrock announced her resignation. She would leave the organisation on 17th November. She had been offered a position as Chief Executive of a voluntary and community sector organisation in North Yorkshire. The Society would for the second time in its history need to find itself a new Managing Director. This time though the organisation was significantly different to the one Stephanie had taken over back in 1998.

The recruitment process to find a new Managing Director took several months but at the end of a long process, the position was offered to Patricia Alexander.

NAMAYIANA

Namayiana Oloshoibor Maasai Women Group.
Namayiana means 'blessed'. Located in a semi-
arid area in Ngong Division of the Kajiado
North District of Kenya. They produce Maasai
beaded jewellery, sandals and blankets

CHAPTER 9
INTERNATIONALISING
THE BUSINESS

"We feel that working with Shared Interest is more than harvest finance, it's a relationship which gives well-being to many families and that is appreciated."
Christian Mora Rojas, Manager of Eco Caraigres 2009

I n the autumn of 2003, the Management Team of Shared Interest met to discuss their plans to move the organisation forward in order to 'Deliver the Vision'. In preparation for the day, Sue Mayo as Business Development Manager wrote her vision for the future of Shared Interest and presented it at this away day:

In five years' time, Shared Interest will be operating with approximately the same number of staff but with a different balance of responsibilities. We will have a sales force located in the field, two covering the Americas, two covering Europe/Africa, two covering Asia/Pacific Rim. They will be supported by six Account Managers located in an office in rural UK, one Account Manager (with fluent language skills relevant to the region they are supporting) per sales staff. A further maximum eight members of staff will be responsible for all non-Sales tasks e.g. Management, Membership, Charity etc. Many key tasks will be outsourced and managed from internally e.g. Accounting, Systems Development, Marketing etc.

Sales staff will be renting desk space in offices shared with other social finance organisations or in service centres set up together with buyer organisations. Partnership arrangements with social finance organisations on key accounts will be occasionally arranged. Product development will be inspired by listening and working alongside our partners in the South and North.

All staff will be recruited for their social motivation and understanding of our vision as well as their ideal skill set. Sales staff will have excellent credit appraisal skills and linguistic abilities appropriate to the region they are operating in. Some may well have commodity-trading experience.

Shared Interest will be recognised as a highly professional specialist finance organisation. Our portfolio will cover a wide number of organisations operating within the fair trade market but will be segmented allowing the organisation to focus on those key accounts that either generate us good levels of income or are key to us for social reasons.

A sister charity will regularly convene meetings with our southern partners arranged perhaps jointly with other social finance organisations to teach, educate and ultimately gather views from those we are seeking to benefit.

While there was much debate over the detail of this vision, the broad idea of expanding the work of Shared Interest to have an international presence, particularly in the developing world, was very much supported. It was recognised that as an organisation, Shared Interest needed to give more voice to its southern partners. Whilst the organisation had been successful in the past at sending out staff from its UK office to visit customers, as the business developed, it became clear that Shared Interest needed to be based alongside its customer base to really understand their needs. Understanding their culture, language and methods of operating were important aspects of giving a voice to Shared Interest's southern partners.

While the lending book had successfully grown over the previous five years, it was acknowledged that the only way there would be continued growth would be through establishing an international presence close to the relevant customers. This close proximity would allow Shared Interest to understand exactly what the customer needed and it was hoped that a close relationship would allow the business to grow.

Towards the end of 2003 Stephanie led the Board through her proposals to develop an international presence for Shared Interest. Firstly she proposed that Shared Interest undertake a period of research looking at re-focusing the customer part of the business towards having locally placed regional staff/contractors. This research was proposed to be completed by March 2004. Then from April 2004 onwards she proposed that Shared Interest pilot/action research to have in post regionally based staff or contractors.

One of the first regions Shared Interest looked at was East Africa. Traidcraft was keen to establish a presence out there and there had been a discussion with Shared Interest about setting up a joint *"service centre"*. This joint service centre approach had been considered when looking at options in India and Bangladesh and although it had not been possible to set it up in those two countries, the proposition was still attractive to both Shared

Interest and Traidcraft. In January 2004 it was confirmed to the Board that the East Africa project with Traidcraft was continuing to develop well.

In Quarterly Return in the autumn of 2004, Shared Interest reported on 'Delivering the vision in Latin America':

In recent months Shared Interest has used two people with direct experience of the needs of producers in Central American countries to find out exactly what financial services would be the most helpful.

The two approaches were quite different. In Costa Rica Shared Interest engaged a consultant specialising in rural finance to produce detailed reports on selected fair trade producers who might benefit from Shared Interest's services. In El Salvador a Traidcraft market access adviser was asked to make contact with a producer organisation which had applied to join the Shared Interest Clearing House.

Shared Interest has engaged Ruth Junkin of the Center for the Competitivity of Eco-Enterprises to visit and research the financial needs of four producer organisations, all certified by FLO, the Fairtrade Labelling Organisation.

At present Ruth has produced two reports: one on a cooperative of banana workers, the other on a larger cooperative of sugar and coffee farmers and other members. Ruth Junkin's main conclusion is that neither of these organisations would benefit from using Shared Interest's credit facilities in the exact way that they are offered at the moment.

Shared Interest asked Sara Velasquez, a market access advisor for Traidcraft, to visit Aprainores, a farmers' association in El Salvador that has been supplying cashew nuts to fair trade buyers for the last eight years. This visit was to be the final step in approving the latest producer member of the Clearing House.

Vicente Carranza is the manager of Aprainores. *"This credit facility from Shared Interest has come just in time as it allows us to leverage a little more working capital from our fair trade clients. We have so many plans for the plant and for the farmers, and access to credit is one of our major limitations."*

As Quarterly Return reported in the autumn of 2005, two new members of staff joined the Business Development Team in late 2004 and early 2005 who were to be critical to the success of developing an international presence:

Ben Lilley, the new Sales Manager has spent most of his life in Africa, most recently working as a national sales manager for a commercial organisation in Gabon. Since joining Shared Interest he has travelled extensively to learn more about the specific financial needs of producers in different countries and fair trade sectors.

Tracy Bonham is responsible for developing long-term projects and, among other things, has been examining the business case for Shared Interest establishing a regional presence in appropriate developing countries.

By October of 2005 Tracy had developed two business cases which were presented to the Board outlining the step by step approach to internationalisation. In the business cases were an explanation of how the costs would increase year on year, but that they were related to the assumptions of sales growth. It was agreed as a first step consultants would be used overseas who would then be able to make a realistic suggestion of sales forecasts for the region.

Clearly within the business cases there were a number of issues to be resolved but the ones that gained the most focus were the size of regions that the international consultants/staff would have to cover and that a large proportion of the work would be in finding suitable partners to work with. The Board did question at the time how feasible it would be to find one person to handle sales work and credit assessment. On the positive side, the fair trade network was acknowledged as being relatively small and well defined which would at least make market assessment relatively easy to manage. It was agreed that it would not necessarily be the task of the consultant to find all the producers themselves.

Almost as important as the regional presence would be the effective follow up and support for new lending opportunities from head office. The post business plan discussion then continued on how growth would be handled particularly by the Customer Service Team. It was anticipated that the capacity of the Customer Service Team to deal with producer and buyer transactions and the administration process associated with greater lending would increase with efficiency gains rather than additional staff.

The autumn 2005 Quarterly Return article went on to report:

Establishing a presence in key regions of the Developing World is part of Shared Interest's plan to internationalise its business and work more closely with producers. The regional staff will have three main roles:
• Increased lending by Shared Interest

- Widening access to fair finance
- Identifying producer groups that would benefit from financial training.

Starting with Africa, Tracy Bonham used information from fair trade organisations, consultants in the field and producer contacts to compare the number of producers involved in fair trade and their credit needs in East, West and Southern Africa. The other sources of finance available in these three regions were also considered. The conclusion was that East Africa is the best potential market for Shared Interest's services at present. In this region the main sources of regulated finance are from microcredit organisations or commercial banks. Neither of these sources meet the needs of medium-size fair trade organisations.

The relative merits of Kenya, Tanzania and Uganda as a location for a regional office were explored. *"Nairobi stood out as the best location for us"* said Tracy. *"Local skills base and infrastructure are good, and there are several like-minded organisations based there."*

A similar research method was used in Latin America. *"Costa Rica was strongly recommended by local consultants"* said Tracy, *"partly because the other countries regard it as the most politically neutral in the region."*

The provisional plans for developing the regional presences in East Africa and Central America involve hiring one or two staff to represent Shared Interest in each region.

"These plans are provisional" said Tracy. *"There are many hurdles to jump. We are more interested in getting a quality solution than a quick one."*

In the autumn of 2005 when the Board discussed the two specific business cases for Kenya and Costa Rica, concerns were expressed about the level of internal capacity to deliver the projects (as Stephanie was working her notice period and Sue Osborne was about to go on maternity leave), and about timing, although it was recognised that there might be a problem with a delay if the business plan projections were to be achieved. There was also a discussion about the level of terms loans and their approval and operation. This was in particular in terms of differentiating the Society from direct competition from other lenders for term loan business. It was noted that there was a market for both term loans and for trade credit and this had been researched and reflected in the business cases. It was accepted that there would need to be a discussion and agreement about the overall prudential policy for controlling exposure to term loans before operations could begin in either area.

To conclude the discussion at this board meeting, the Moderator, Philip Angier confirmed that the East Africa project was approved as set out in the business case. Phase one of the Central America project was approved – get the regional presence up and running with a long-term consultant contract in place but a further board discussion would be needed before phase two, formal recruitment of a member of staff and establishing an office, was approved. The Directors also expressed a desire to find ways of reducing costs of setting up, particularly in Africa, perhaps by sharing accommodation with Traidcraft or others.

A significant amount of work was then undertaken after achieving Board approval to establish the regional presences and finally Quarterly Return in the spring of 2006 included in its AGM report information on the 'staff recruited in Kenya and Costa Rica':

Shared Interest's plans to internationalise its business have moved forward significantly with the recruitment of Rachel Ngondo and Hugo Villela. In the coming months they will be developing a regional presence for Shared Interest in East Africa and Latin America.

Hugo Villela has been working as Shared Interest's representative in Latin America since early February. He has already held face-to-face meetings with several producer groups to discuss their credit needs. He introduced himself to Shared Interest members in a video message, which also showed him meeting members of the Coopecañera sugar cooperative.

Rachel Ngondo starts work in April. One of her first tasks will be to attend the COFTA (Co-operation of Fair Trade in Africa) conference in Arusha, Tanzania. Shared Interest will be sharing the office in Nairobi, as well as resources and support staff with Traidcraft, a long-term partner of Shared Interest.

In May 2006 the Board spent some time seeking to improve their understanding of the benefits and risks of the regional presence of Shared Interest. It was noted that it was an integral part of the Delivering the Vision project, previously discussed and approved by the Directors over 18 months ago when the project was initiated. A detailed analysis of the risks identified at the time of the Project Initiation Document was being maintained by Tracy and her team and an up to date monitoring report was being produced regularly.

Tracy reported on the depth of analysis that had been undertaken stressing that the route chosen to establish the regional presences was for Shared Interest to have an office in each country but only one legal entity in the UK rather than establishing independent companies in each jurisdiction. This was after significant research had been undertaken to understand the legal limitations placed on operating in each country.

One of the Directors noted that induction into an organisation was very important and shouldn't be seen as a one-off event but part of a continuing programme of development. The benefits of using indigenous staff in overseas locations are that indigenous staff members know things that HQ staff can't possibly know and will also be able to do things that HQ staff can't do. The challenge is how to get the best from these benefits. It was felt best to avoid having only one point of contact in any territory so that communication does not become restricted to one channel.

It would be good, the Board felt for Rachel Ngondo in Kenya and Hugo Villela to spend some time together so they can share their experiences and learn more quickly about being part of the Shared Interest team. It was felt important for remote staff to have the opportunity to visit the team in the UK and perhaps they should be invited to attend the AGM each year and also attend the board meeting that precedes the AGM.

As it happened an enormous amount of effort was put into the induction of both Hugo and Rachel, by both Ben Lilley and Malcolm Curtis. Both travelled out to their respective regions and spent time with them in the UK, ensuring they were fully integrated into the staff team and ways of working at Shared Interest.

By the summer of 2006, Hugo was already showing his worth, as was reported in Quarterly Return:

Shared Interest's representative in Latin America, Hugo Villela, has been very busy over the last six months. He has handled enquiries for finance from 25 fair trade producer groups in El Salvador, Costa Rica, Honduras, Nicaragua, Bolivia, Chile and Peru and he has made 13 site visits. The great majority of the groups are food producers – coffee, pineapples, sugar, bananas, and cashew nuts – although there have been two enquiries from handicraft producers.

"My job is to be a bridge between poor producers and investors at Shared Interest" said Hugo. *"I like to bring people closer together. What I particularly like about Shared Interest is that the money comes from the savings of normal people – it's not grants."*

At the board meeting in March 2007, Rachel Ngondo and Hugo Villela were able to attend with Ben Lilley and give their views on how the regional offices were working. Rachel shared how much learning there had been for her in the last 12 months; learning about producers, their products and also about Shared Interest. One of the challenges of her role was working with producers who have incomplete financial records, perhaps in Swahili. Communicating with producers and obtaining financial information was a major challenge.

Hugo's background was in agronomy. He felt his work with Shared Interest was an opportunity to see solutions to problems in relatively short time periods rather than some of the long term projects that his other work has involved. Customers in Central America were very interested in the cooperative, 8,500 member nature of the Society. This gave the Society a unique place in the market. One of the strangest things to Hugo was that inside the Society we think of ourselves as a small initiative whereas outside the Society we are seen as a large, effective player.

Rachel felt that term loans were likely to be the growth area in Africa but Hugo was more impressed with the lower potential risk presented by the provision of working capital finance.

Ben at the time noted that East Africa had a long way to go before it matched Central America in terms of financial sophistication. Despite initial fears from producers about increasing costs the Society's presence in East Africa had been welcomed.

In Quarterly Return in the winter of 2006/7, Shared Interest reported on a 'rush of proposals from regional offices':

Both Shared Interest's overseas executives, Rachel Ngondo in Kenya and Hugo Villela in Costa Rica, have started 2007 with a mass of credit and loan applications to prepare.

At the end of 2006 Rachel visited two tea producer groups in Uganda. One needs finance to purchase a tea estate from the government and the other is considering a smaller loan to buy a generator. She is also helping another tea producer group, in Kenya, to prepare a proposal to buy a factory. Following her visit with Ben Lilley to the Kisii district of Kenya in October, she is working on credit applications for three more producer groups in this area famous for soapstone carving.

Hugo Villela went to Honduras and El Salvador in December. In Honduras he visited five coffee cooperatives and he will be preparing loan applications for two of them. In El Salvador he made a follow-up visit to an existing customer, Aprainores – an association of 130 cashew nut farmers who revived an abandoned estate. Also in El Salvador Hugo visited a cooperative of over 250 artisans who produce a wide variety of crafts, including embroidered clothing, jewellery, hammocks, bags and wooden crafts. As a result he is preparing his first credit application for a handicraft producer group.

Hugo moved offices in December to a more commercial part of San Jose. Meanwhile in Nairobi, Rachel says that Fair Trade House, which is shared by Shared Interest, Traidcraft and COFTA (the African Fair Trade Association) is becoming the centre of a lot of activity and is excellent for networking. Rachel will be representing Shared Interest at the World Social Forum in Nairobi at the end of January.

At the 17th Annual General Meeting held on 24th March 2007 in London, Hugo and Rachel welcomed the opportunity to talk about their work and in particular answer questions from members. This was reported on in Quarterly Return Issue 63:

Answering questions by members, Rachel said that fair trade organisations were very aware of the problems faced by handicraft producers and the need for them to adapt to the changing demands of export markets. COFTA (the African Fair Trade Association which has offices in the same premises as Shared Interest in Nairobi) is running a programme to encourage producer groups to work with designers. Hugo said there were similar problems in Central America, and some handicraft groups were diversifying into agriculture.

Both Hugo and Rachel gave examples of the impact Shared Interest is having. Hugo explained that many farmers would find it impossible to borrow money without security, and in Bolivia and El Salvador the local banks do not lend to agricultural businesses at all. Rachel described how a small credit facility of £5,000 for the Yatta South Women's Group was making a huge difference to the lives of some 2,000 basket weavers in Kenya. With a secure income and no need to borrow from local moneylenders the group was able to invest more money in education and community facilities.

At the board meeting in October 2007, Will Cowell, Project Leader made a presentation on the South America regional presence business case. It was noted that Hugo Villela's contract in Costa Rica was in the process of being converted to a legal representative in the same way that was proposed to be an outcome of the South America proposal.

The proposal to open an office in South America was reported on in Quarterly Return in the winter of 2007/8:

The strategy to develop a better understanding of the needs of producers by employing staff based in specific regions of the world has been so successful that Shared Interest is preparing to open an office in South America during 2008.

"It's fair to say that without Hugo and Rachel on the ground we would never have approved so many proposals nor would the value have been so high," says Customer Services Director Malcolm Curtis. *"Some of the proposals have been particularly complicated and some have introduced us to new markets."*

"Our whole profile has increased," says Commercial Manager Ben Lilley. *"Whereas in the past people had never heard of Shared Interest,*

today they are seeking us out because of the reputation built by the regional commercial team. We are fast becoming the name that buyers and producers in Fair Trade turn to before considering other finance because they know we will listen to their needs and address them in a fair and transparent manner."

Shared Interest plans to build on this success by recruiting a Market Development Executive for South America and opening an office in Lima, Peru. The fair trade market in Peru is relatively well developed and Shared Interest has several customers and contacts there. Having an office there will also help Hugo in Central America by having a colleague based in the same time zone.

"A local executive can be the bridge between the cultural differences in Latin America and the UK and the language differences too," says Hugo. *"And I'm available for most part of Latin America working hours. That means I can have good communication with clients during the day, and they know they can call me to discuss any arising points."*

In March 2008 Hugo and Rachel were welcomed back into the board room ahead of the AGM the following day. Rachel was able to tell the Board that she had travelled widely throughout East Africa in the last year. The Society's approach was being welcomed by producer customers. Problems in Kenya following the election violence in January 2008 had been *"quite scary"* with some producers having problems caused by transport difficulties which were taking time to resolve.

Hugo for his part, confirmed he felt more like a *"proper member"* of the Society's family. He felt he now had a closer relationship with the staff of the Society. The whole business for him depended on building relationships but the relationship between Hugo and the rest of the staff was the first building block. The Central American business continued to grow rapidly and Hugo's contacts in the fair trade networks in Central America were developing.

Hugo and Rachel both expressed a desire to the Board to become investors in the Society and it was agreed that they should be allowed to become members.

One of the Directors asked the Regional Development Executives how rising commodity prices and the US slowdown were affecting producers. Rachel responded that fuel costs had risen by 20% in Kenya since January 2008. Producers on fixed price contracts, especially coffee producers, were finding the situation challenging and some contracts would have to be renegotiated. There was a challenge for producers when information about market trends was not easily available. Hugo explained that high and unstable coffee prices were being experienced in Central America. The key problem was about how the price was fixed in the contract. Training from TWIN (a UK based fair trade organisation dedicated to improving the fair trade supply chain for commodity producers) was helping many producers to solve the problem and some producers were finding a benefit in changing to Euros from US dollars.

At the AGM the following day, once again contributions made by Rachel and Hugo were much appreciated by members, judging by comments on their feedback forms. Quarterly Return Issue 67 reported:

Both of them described how their work involved visiting producer groups, listening to their needs and where appropriate helping them to apply for finance. Rachel said that many of the groups she helped did not have the skills to fill out an application form. Hugo said that most of the groups he worked with had good financial information but were reluctant to share it with him until he had gained their trust.

In both regions finance from Shared Interest was having a big impact and some additional benefits that they had not expected. Rachel explained how managing a Shared Interest credit facility made producer groups more efficient with their administration. Some commercial buyers had told her that they preferred to deal with Shared Interest customers because they were more professional. Hugo said that he knew of examples of customers who had been offered improved terms by local banks who were impressed by the backing from a group of UK private investors.

In Quarterly Return in the spring of 2009, Shared Interest reported on 'Our man in Lima':

Shared Interest has opened an office in Lima, Peru and has appointed local resident Paul Sablich, 30 as the Regional Development Executive for South America. This expansion builds on the success of the regional offices in Kenya and Costa Rica opened in 2006.

South America has enormous potential for Shared Interest to grow its business and increase the social impact it has. Shared Interest already has nine customers in Peru, and there are at least another 85 Fair Trade producer groups in the country, which is one of the reasons why Peru was chosen as the regional base. There are well over 300 potential new customers in the whole of South America.

"Peru is a very unequal society with a huge gap between the rich and the poor," said Paul. *"Fair Trade makes perfect sense. It's a tool to generate equity in the world. I want to be part of the solution and help to create the right environment for Fair Trade to take place."*

Elisabeth Wilson, who is Paul's manager in the UK, said: *"We are expecting the new regional office to become financially self-sufficient within three years. However, we believe that we will start to increase our social impact in the region immediately.*

"We have noticed that some of our existing customers in South America are making greater use of their Shared Interest credit facilities as local banks are restricting lending. There are already seven possible new applications for lending for Paul to progress.

"There's huge demand for Shared Interest's fair lending, but we need much more investment from existing and new members to satisfy that demand."

In March 2009 the Business Development Team including the Regional Development Executives all joined the board meeting. They were able to say that there were plenty of proposals in the pipeline but there was concern at the limitations imposed by the *"drying up"* of loans because of the breach of the prudential limit. It was noted that the SCAA conference was coming up and the sales team would be under a great deal of pressure. It was suggested that stock facilities (short term loans, less than one year) might help ease seasonality in the Society's portfolio of loans.

At the AGM the following day, the International Team were once again popular with the members who attended. The AGM was reported on in Quarterly Return Issue 71:

"In East Africa the overall situation is grim" said Rachel Ngondo. *"Economic growth is falling and inflation and interest rates are rising. Interest rates of over 20% on loans are common."*

She said that the outlook was surprisingly good for the region's leading exports: tea, coffee, agricultural and horticultural products. However the reduction in purchasing power in Europe and US had resulted in low demand for handicraft exports. Some handicraft producers were reporting a 40% drop in orders.

She said that Shared Interest now had a well established presence in East Africa. When she first started in 2006 she had to spend a lot of time going out and telling people about Shared Interest. Now she gets plenty of enquiries.

Hugo Villela said that exporters in Central America were experiencing similar difficulties with restricted credit and rising interest rates: *"Ethical businesses are the solution. Fair trade is the model. Shared Interest is leading the way,"* he said.

He said that Shared Interest had good 'brand recognition' among fair trade producers as a financial services provider with fair lending terms. Shared Interest was doing more than just lending money, he said. In building a relationship with producers he could provide business advice where needed, apply pressure on other ethical lenders to improve their terms, and enable fair trade producers to enter international commodities markets.

After an exciting transition from a solely UK-based organisation to one with a presence in three regions, it is exciting to look forward to a future when further offices will increase Shared Interest's international presence.

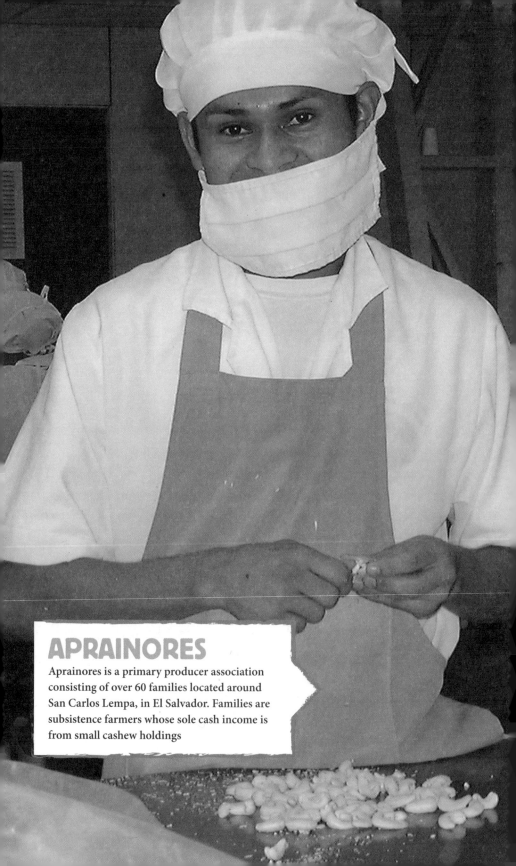

APRAINORES

Aprainores is a primary producer association consisting of over 60 families located around San Carlos Lempa, in El Salvador. Families are subsistence farmers whose sole cash income is from small cashew holdings

CHAPTER 10
ESTABLISHING A
CHARITY

"The difference it makes is simple, it enables us as a business to gain the basic knowledge needed to ensure we grow, which in turn means that we can support a larger number of marginalized producers enabling them to provide for their families, put food on the table, send their children to school, put a roof over their heads and afford health care. We're not asking for hand outs, but what we are asking for is your support to lift ourselves out of poverty, the support (training) provided by Shared Interest Foundation will help us to achieve this."
Anne Nzilani, Product Development Manager for Mango True Mirage, Kenya

———◆———

Shared Interest right from inception has always had charitable status on the agenda. It had been ruled out early on when it was acknowledged it would be too restrictive. However, staff at Shared Interest returned again to the idea of a charity in 2002 and in July of that year at the annual strategic review, there was a debate by the Board as to whether to establish a charity.

The rationale for establishing a charity included the following:

- It would be easier to attract grants and donations to the Foundation rather than the Society, which would enable projects to proceed quicker than they would otherwise
- The Foundation would be explicitly authorised to provide education while the Society only has the power to provide money for education out of profits
- It would be a tax-efficient way to use the Society's profits, enabling Shared Interest as a whole to be of greater assistance to producers in the Developing World
- Some potential partners, particularly NGOs and charities, e.g. the Fairtrade Foundation, would find it easier to work with another charity.

The paper to the Board confirmed that the principle of distributing profit for charitable purposes was in the rules of the Society and therefore was generally favoured. A paper was presented arguing the case for a dedicated Shared Interest Charity, a development requested by some members of the Society.

At the time, there was significant discussion about the reasons for and against the establishment of a charity. It was noted that there were many development charities already in existence and before agreeing to establish a charity, it was important to be clear on how a Shared Interest charity might add value and if established what would be its unique contribution? It was agreed that Shared Interest could consider where possible working with others to deliver projects or programmes.

It was recognised that where Shared Interest might add value would be in the area of projects, such as setting up a 'Shared Interest' in Bangladesh, an idea for which at the time no suitable existing charity seemed to exist.

Of course governance was debated at length, in particular the constituents of any Board of Trustees of a charity and the extent to which there should be overlap with the Board of the Society. Within this discussion, it was also considered what the possible objects of a charity should be.

After a lengthy debate, it was agreed that the Management of Shared Interest be empowered to consult with legal experts on the possibility of establishing a sister charity, the results of which would be reported to the Board and the Board would then decide whether to put the proposal to members at the 2003 Annual General Meeting.

The Board debated the charity again early in 2003 and it confirmed the process and timetable for establishing a charity. The Board agreed to the principle of having a sister charity but whether it should be a simple trust or a company limited by guarantee was not settled. It was agreed that the Management Team should gain further legal advice on this point and bring a draft constitution back to the Board.

The report on the 2003 AGM which featured in Quarterly Return, quotes that the: *"AGM approved a resolution to set aside £10,000 for charitable purposes"*. The MD clarified that: *"The Directors were planning to set up a 'sister' charity to Shared Interest,"* as *"the charity will enable us to do new things related to our existing work, for example educational work, capacity building and providing services that would not otherwise be financially viable."*

In the spring of 2003 a new set of papers from the lawyers was circulated to the Board and it was agreed that the Society should be the founding and only member of a charitable company, to be called the Shared Interest Foundation. There was a discussion about the distinction between objects and powers and the best way to present the list of activities the Society would like to undertake. It was agreed that further advice should be sought on this but that they should be set as wide as possible. The Directors of the Society should be the Trustees of the charity, if possible. A committee of the Moderator, Managing Director, Finance Director and the Secretary was delegated to finalise the documentation, obtaining legal advice as necessary, and to register the charity with the relevant authorities.

On 19th November 2003, the Trustees agreed to the opening of a Bank Account for the Shared Interest Foundation and completed the Charity Registration Application form.

By the summer of 2004, the Board had a pre-business plan discussion about the Foundation. Stuart Raistrick, Company Secretary, introduced the paper which was intended as the pre-cursor of a business plan setting out the main ideas about initial projects for the Foundation and recommending that fundraising should build on the established behaviour of members. The possible transfer of waived interest to the Foundation was not included in the budget that was approved at the same meeting.

It was agreed the £10,000 set aside for charitable purposes as agreed by members at the 2003 AGM would be given to the Foundation. This was reported on in Quarterly Return Issue 51 in the spring of 2004:

Last year members agreed at the AGM to set aside £10,000 for charitable purposes. The Directors have recently set up a charitable company called Shared Interest Foundation. Stephanie said that this would play an important supporting role to the main business of the Society. It might, for example fund things that would otherwise be uneconomic, add value for producers or strengthen the fair trade movement.

At the time of agreeing this, it was also agreed that the Foundation would become a member of the Fairtrade Foundation, a position that was only available to charitable organisations. Membership came at an annual cost of £5,000 made up of a membership fee of £500 and grants towards Fairtrade

Foundation projects of up to £4,500. It was agreed that each project would be presented to Trustees for approval before any funds were released. Engaging in this way with the Fairtrade Foundation opened up many opportunities for Shared Interest as a whole and it was seen as a positive move.

By the time of the board meeting prior to the 2005 AGM it had also been agreed to pay £84,713 from the reserve for charitable purposes to the Shared Interest Foundation on 14th March 2005 subject to approval at the AGM.

In her speech to the AGM, Stephanie confirmed that: *"We have now set up our sister charity, the Shared Interest Foundation, which will carry out work to improve access to fair finance and develop capacity and skills with marginalised producers. As a first act, however, the Foundation used some of its initial money to assist producer organisations affected by the Tsunami on Boxing Day."*

The expenditure of £3,000 on grants to help in the relief effort following the Tsunami on 26th December 2004 had been reported on in Quarterly Return earlier in the year:

In the first 10 days following the disaster, the Foundation made three donations to organisations requesting emergency assistance from partners and we will respond to any other requests we receive. In the long term, we aim to work with our partner networks in fair trade and the cooperative movement to assist with reconstruction and development and will report on any progress on this.

At the March 2005 board meeting, Sue Osborne introduced the business plan that had been prepared. There was some discussion around the detail of the projects forming the plan and on the principles behind the plan particularly the governance of the Foundation and its relationship with the Society.

Some challenged the idea that the regional presence and commodity projects could be funded by the Foundation – some Trustees felt they were *"business as usual"* for the Society and not *"charitable"*. The importance of the Foundation keeping within its charitable objects was stressed.

In the end, it was agreed to approve in part the expenditure proposed on both the East Africa project and the Central America project. It was further agreed to approve expenditure on the commodity project up to £20,000.

At the time, there was a proposal that the Foundation should review its board membership with a view to including *"independent"* Trustees, that is to say Trustees with no other connection with the Society. It was agreed that this proposal should be discussed at a future meeting of Trustees.

The Secretary explained that he was taking advice about appointing new executive directors of the Society to be Trustees of the Foundation. Present policy of the Trustees, to have common directors with the Society, would require this but there might be legal difficulties. He agreed to produce a paper on the subject with recommendations in due course.

When the first business plan for the Foundation was returned to the Trustees in May 2005 it was approved. It was noted that members should be given the opportunity to donate to the Foundation but there would not be an immediate push for donations until a communications strategy had been agreed. The fundraising plan had already begun and would be the priority for the next few weeks. This was developed in a piece in Quarterly Return later in the year when legacies to the Foundation were promoted:

As you may be aware, Shared Interest Society recently established a sister charity called Shared Interest Foundation. The creation of the

Foundation allows us to strengthen the impact of our work and achieve our vision of making real and lasting improvements to the lives of disadvantaged producers.

We believe the Foundation will complement our existing offering of financial services by increasing our support for producers. The Foundation will provide training around business financial management and skill development, as well as widening access to fair finance. Providing the lending needed to support trade sometimes is not enough and help with financial training or with skills development is also needed. We have a network of contacts and enough experience to ensure that our help will be targeted where it will achieve real benefits.

Over the last fifteen years your investments have allowed us to provide financial services to fair trade organisations all around the world. We would now like to invite you to consider extending your support to the Foundation.

For those of you interested in supporting this work, we would ask you to consider taking one very simple action. You could make a provision, that upon your death, your investment in Shared Interest Society Limited be converted into a donation for the charity Shared Interest Foundation.

Leaving a legacy in this way will ensure that the producers you have helped in the past will continue to benefit long into the future.

This article received an encouraging response from members and showed their support to the work of the Foundation.

Back in the spring of 2005, the Trustees returned again to the governance debate as there was a concern that the Foundation was too closely linked to the Society. Stuart Raistrick, Company Secretary presented a paper discussing the governance of the Foundation.

It was envisaged that the Foundation and Society would work alongside each other. This was a strength and not a weakness as both were working in the same areas for the same people. It was noted that the Charity Commission had agreed the formation of the Foundation and its governing documents.

The idea of having independent non-execs on the Foundation's Board was discussed in the light of possible future conflicts of interest, for example fundraising from members. It was noted that other organisations such as Traidcraft have the same Board for both their business and charity.

By the end of 2005, the Trustees took an exciting step when they authorised expenditure of £17,400 on the Producer Training Project. This was the first spending on what is now the focus of the Foundation's activities.

In Quarterly Return in the winter of 2005, the Foundation reported on other proposed expenditure:

Shared Interest's sister charity, the Shared Interest Foundation, is to sponsor the Fairtrade Foundation's producer tour during Fairtrade Fortnight, March 2006. This will be the latest project the Foundation has funded, having assisted producer organisations affected by the Tsunami in 2004.

Fairtrade Fortnight is a key event in the annual campaigning calendar providing fantastic opportunities to raise awareness of fair trade to new audiences, deepen understanding among existing supporters and ultimately increase sales of fair trade products. One of the highlights will be the producer tour, when fair trade producers come over to the UK to attend locally organised events across the country.

Early in 2006, Tracy Bonham, Projects Manager gave a presentation on the budget and fundraising for the Foundation. To progress the work of the Foundation an application was being prepared in conjunction with the Coops College to Comic Relief and the Board asked that they be kept up to date on the application. As it happened Comic Relief turned the application down, with a lack of track record as the primary reason. With regard to fundraising from individuals it was noted that that building and managing relationships was key, and ideally the Foundation should have a mix of small and large potential donors.

Quarterly Return in the summer of 2006 reported on another milestone. The first major project of the Shared Interest Foundation – a business skills training course held with a producer group, Mango True Mirage, in Kenya which had been undertaken to respond to the feedback from Comic Relief that the Foundation needed a proven track record of producer training:

Mango True Mirage is a private limited company established in 1998 by skilled craftsmen and women from economically marginalised groups in Kenya.

Its mission is to work with marginalised groups by marketing their products in order to alleviate poverty and improve their lives and to educate their members that alternative trade will make them economically independent.

Through the Foundation's training Mango True Mirage will be able to strengthen its business and implement a number of significant changes to help build a sustainable business. This will directly benefit all its 2,000 producers and their families and communities.

"It's like finding hidden gems. I never knew the resources I had

and how much untapped knowledge there was among my staff," Beth Wambua, General Manager.

In the same edition, Shared Interest staff reported on the effort they were making to raise funds for Shared Interest Foundation. A group of employees and members cycled the challenging sea-to-sea route to raise funds. The group completed the 140 miles from one side of England to the other side in just two-and-a-half days, along a route which took in the northern Lake District before climbing the Pennines and then descending to the railway paths of County Durham. As well as this internal fundraising effort, the Foundation was also successful at sourcing a number of small grants which eased the disappointment of being turned down by Comic Relief.

Meanwhile back in the office there was still debate over how the regional presence costs should be split between the Society and the Foundation. The implementation costs had been covered by the Foundation in 2006 but it was agreed that in the future, implementation costs for new regional presences would have to be met from the Society. It was noted that regional staff members would have roles in both the Society and the Foundation and there would be regular reviews of the recharges to make sure the costs were located in the correct organisation.

Finally it was noted that the original intention of the Foundation was to provide an outlet for any *"surplus"* profit of the Society and this explained the assumption in the Society business plan that a proportion of profits would be given to the Foundation.

In the autumn of 2006, Quarterly Return reported on an exciting piece of news – a coffee cooperative that had benefited from both the Foundation and the Society:

Shared Interest's work with Gumutindo Coffee Cooperative in Uganda is a good example of how the activities of the Society and Foundation complement each other.

Gumutindo is a secondary (or marketing) cooperative owned by six producer cooperatives with a total of 2,500 members. For many years it has supplied premium quality Fair Trade coffee to Twin (and Cafédirect). Last year the cooperative had to vacate its leased warehouse. It found a suitable warehouse to purchase but it needed renovation, which Gumutindo was able to do with the help of a five year loan from Shared Interest.

As a result of this contact Gumutindo learned of the work of Shared Interest Foundation and in August this year its manager received training in accounting skills co-funded by the Foundation and Cafédirect.

This financial training will not only improve the management of the cooperative. It also improves the 'risk profile' which Shared Interest uses when considering loan applications. Which means that in future Gumutindo should be able to borrow more money from Shared Interest.

This example also illustrates how the producer, the buyer (TWIN) and Shared Interest worked together to make fair trade operate as effectively as possible.

In October 2006, the trustees meeting began with a short video that had been prepared as an introduction to the Foundation. After the presentation the Trustees complimented staff that the presentation had been very helpful and had articulated the distinctive contributions and focus of the Foundation in relation to the current business plan.

At the same meeting, the Trustees then began an exercise to try and establish the three most pressing issues surrounding the Foundation and its objectives. The main issue to emerge from this was a need to review and possibly regularise some governance matters. In particular there is a need to consider the role of the Managing Trustee and whether this should be a paid position. In due course a further discussion about whether there should be an independent director unconnected with Shared Interest Society would also be explored.

There was also caution expressed about referring to the Society and Foundation combined as one organisation and it was suggested that the organisation should always refer to *"Shared Interest"* when it meant to include both the Society and the Foundation.

Also in October 2006, Andrea Wilkinson, in her Foundation role, wrote a paper to the Board detailing what she perceived as the key challenges for the Foundation at the time and ultimately it served to remind the Board what the purpose of the Foundation was. She explained to the Board that they had appointed a fundraising consultant who had assisted them in both developing a successful fundraising strategy and raising funds. She acknowledged that the generosity of Shared Interest members had been overwhelming – with over two thirds of the overall fundraising goal achieved in three months, in total more than £32,300 of the £40,000 target. In addition to covering some core costs, this money was identified for use in training over 80 fair trade producer groups in Africa.

Another challenge for the Foundation, Andrea felt, was the fact that it had taken too low a priority in the past, as it was essentially not 'core business'. She was hopeful that the complementary role that had always been identified for the Foundation alongside the Society, would start to come to fruition in situations like for example when staff are carrying out due diligence with producers, they can at the same time identify other issues that the Foundation might be able to address through its capacity work.

The last key challenge that Andrea focused on in her paper was the lack of clarity between the Society and the Foundation, an issue that both the Board and staff have had concerns about. With the staff, this has been worked through at various briefing sessions and staff had already demonstrated greater buy-in through their initiation and implementation of fundraising events, such as the Coast-to-Coast cycle ride. Taking on board the feedback from numerous Board and staff discussions it had been decided that the Foundation would no longer carry out any of the implementation of the regional presence projects.

In Andrea's paper she confirmed her view of how the Society and Foundation complemented each other in a table, which is copied below:

Society	Foundation
Sales focused research	Research of benefit to the wider community
Lending to producers	Grants for producers
Producer capacity building through loans	Producer capacity building through training
Support the fair trade movement by providing loans to buyers	Support to the fair trade movement by grant support e.g. the Fairtrade Foundation

In Quarterly Return in the winter 2006/7 issue, the Foundation reported on the first training course outside of Kenya:

This was an intensive training programme with the only IFAT registered fair trade organisation in Rwanda, called Dancing Pots.

This innovative pottery project was established in 2001 and works with 14 groups of Twa people (sometimes known as pygmies) located throughout Rwanda. By commercialising the Twa's traditional skills of pottery and dance, and creating a Twa-run fair trade enterprise, Dancing Pots is helping to reduce poverty and social exclusion.

Pottery is a traditional Twa craft in Rwanda and is culturally important. However, as originally practised it is often a loss-making exercise. The training delivered by Shared Interest Foundation was vital for Dancing Pots and will assist them in working in an integrated way on key aspects of business development with potters, including: marketing; business planning; financial management; helping the organisation to become a sustainable and profitable business.

Before the training Dancing Pots did not have a business plan. Now the Manager of Dancing Pots, Jean Munyaneza, feels able to prepare one. He said: *"A business plan for me will be like glasses to someone who is short sighted – it will help me look so far and see the future of my business."*

Early in 2007 at the Trustees meeting, it was confirmed that the Fairtrade Foundation media tour was being supported by the Foundation and Gail Porter and some journalists were being taken to Gumutindo in Uganda, the coffee cooperative that had been reported on in Quarterly Return the previous year. It had been hoped that Rachel Ngondo would have been able to join the visit but that did not prove possible.

Gail's trip to eastern Uganda secured significant media coverage for fair trade and the benefits it brings to Gumutindo's farmers. Shared Interest has loaned funds to Gumutindo Cooperative for the acquisition and renovation of a coffee warehouse and offices.

Gail visited the home of cooperative treasurer Oliva Kishera in Buginyanya. Oliva, like thousands of others in Uganda, is a smallholder coffee farmer who cultivates, harvests and processes coffee on her 'shamba' or plot (typically the size of an average UK back garden). She is proud to use organic farming methods.

With the additional income from fair trade, Oliva has been able to pay for her children to attend school, providing them with opportunities she did not have. She told Gail: *"I want my children to be educated, as I want them to have more opportunities and a better future. Being able to educate my children is one of the biggest achievements of my life."*

Oliva added: *"Fair trade has encouraged the participation of women in our organisation and now women's voices are recognised at all the Gumutindo meetings. There are even more women than men in the Gumutindo team. Fair trade has helped make the dream of women come true."*

Oliva is now the treasurer of the Gumutindo Cooperative. This is a really big step for Oliva and women in her region as, traditionally, men dominated positions of power. Oliva was the first female to sit on the Gumutindo Board, and today the Board has equal male and female representation.

Gail Porter's visit to Uganda sparked a number of letters from members into the Editor of Quarterly Return:

Funding celebrity

In view of my total disenchantment with the celebrity culture in the UK, Gail Porter's visit to the Gumutindo coffee cooperative has put me off any further donations to Shared Interest Foundation.

How can the Foundation justify funding a presumably affluent TV presenter (thereby increasing her carbon footprint) when I think the money could be better spent helping producers get a rung up onto the fair trade ladder? I would be interested to know where all the claimed publicity was used besides in QR.

Margaret Vernon, York

Editor replies:

The visit by Gail Porter and reporters to East Africa was organised by the Fairtrade Foundation and funded by Shared Interest Foundation which covered the travel and accommodation expenses. Gail Porter was not paid for her participation.

Shared Interest Foundation is one of the 'charity shareholders' of the Fairtrade Foundation and this arrangement involves an element of funding. By financing this media tour Shared Interest Foundation fulfilled its obligation and gained publicity for Shared Interest and for one of its producer customers.

This tour resulted in coverage in three national newspapers and on BBC TV. There were also many mentions in other media.

By the summer of 2007, the Board was told about applications to Comic Relief, the Big Lottery Fund and some possible work with the Fairtrade

Foundation and Quarterly Return in the autumn of 2007 was reporting on more activities undertaken by the Foundation: a training course in Harare, Zimbabwe for 30 craft producers; a grant to Fairtrade banana farmers in the Windward Islands who had lost their crops as a result of Hurricane Dean and the third in a series of training courses being delivered across Africa, the latest of which was in South Africa.

The next edition of Quarterly Return in the winter of 2007/8 went into more detail:

These new training initiatives will build on the success of the programmes developed in 2006/7 when Shared Interest Foundation worked with seventy-one producer groups in five countries throughout Africa. The groups ranged from basket weavers in Rwanda to soapstone carvers in Kenya to jewellery makers in South Africa.

The training included financial and business skills courses, fair trade awareness workshops and product development seminars.

The programme for Rwanda, which is the more advanced, will involve three levels of learning suitable for producer groups at different stages of development. Level one will benefit producer groups that are already exporting. Level three will be suitable for informal groups that are just thinking about selling. We hope these groups will move through all three levels during the three year programme.

It was then with great excitement in Quarterly Return in the spring of 2008 that the Foundation was able to report it had been awarded £236,000 by the Big Lottery Fund to train fair trade producers in Rwanda through the three year programme detailed above. This elevated the work of the Foundation to another level and this grant was celebrated by staff and Board alike.

"This programme could have a very significant impact in a small, underdeveloped country like Rwanda," said Andrea Wilkinson, Project Leader for the Foundation. *"We estimate that 9,000 people will benefit directly from the training. Plus there is the wider benefit of building a strong fairtrade network."*

It was reported that the Foundation would be finalising the details of the training programme and would be recruiting a local manager and trainers in preparation for the first training course to start in January 2009.

With the project in Rwanda funded and being progressed, attention was then moved to Swaziland and this was reported on in Quarterly Return in the autumn of 2008:

During her intensive three-week journey Andrea Wilkinson had 20 meetings with a wide range of groups including glass blowers, candle makers, basket weavers, jewellery makers, souvenir sellers, wine makers and chocolatiers. She visited the largest trade fair in the southern hemisphere and delivered five training sessions to a total of 100 people from three countries.

Those individuals interested in monitoring Andrea's progress were able to read more about her journey on a business blog which was sponsored by a local newspaper in Newcastle.

At the 2009 AGM, Andrea was able to report on another successful year for the Foundation. During the course of the year prior, the Foundation had trained 167 producer groups and over 250 people in 7 countries. It had trained over 40% of all IFAT registered businesses in Africa.

In the summer of 2009, Quarterly Return reported on the first year of Big Lottery Funded producer training:

"The evaluation trip was a great success, it was incredibly exciting for us to mark the end of the first year of this project and to start seeing the results," said Andrea. *"And what results they were! All of the tier one producer organisations (many of whom are already exporting their goods) are developing business plans and have made great strides in updating and developing their financial systems."*

The 10 days ended with a graduation ceremony that acknowledged the endless hours of hard work and commitment put in by the trainers. They had completed training in business skills and 'training for trainers' from our project partners Traidcraft, and they had also developed a comprehensive training manual that is specific to Rwandan small to medium sized enterprises and will be used throughout the three years of the project and beyond.

One of the trainers, Yves, said in his speech: *"This is the beginning for us to put into practice what we have learnt, we will train all of the 50 producer organisations and help them to change their businesses for the better, to make more profit, to run more efficiently and to make a difference to the lives of their cooperative members and workers. This is the beginning and we will see it through to the end."*

In July 2009 the Board heard that the Foundation's role was evolving from that of training the producers to that of training the trainers and becoming more involved in research and evaluation. The Trustees went on to discuss fundraising and it was suggested that funding applications to other Charitable

Foundations had significantly decreased due to the recession and therefore this might be an opportune time to approach them for funding.

Clearly the Foundation has proved itself to be an exciting addition to the work of the Society. As Michael Walton, former Board member commented: *"The Foundation is a very good development and builds on the knowledge of Shared Interest. The people driving the Foundation forward have demonstrated that they really know what is needed and are out there providing that service. It is highly commendable. The credibility of the Shared Interest Foundation, through the grants it has secured and the work that is being delivered, is brilliant and a real asset to Shared Interest as a whole."*

GETRADE FPS

Getrade Fair Trade Producer's Society in Accra, Ghana was founded in 1986. It acts as an export house for traditional handicraft producers and small farmers producing baskets, carved wooden toys and furniture, and herbal teas

CHAPTER 11
A NEW MANAGING
DIRECTOR

"When I was first on the board we had the money, but we hadn't spent enough of it...we were trying to think of ways to spend it. Now here we are fully lent, it's been a complete turnaround, now as Shared Interest and fair trade has grown we have so many people/producers that desperately need the money and not enough money to lend out to them."

Michael Walton, former Board member

At the first board meeting of the year in February 2006, Philip Angier welcomed the third Managing Director of Shared Interest, Patricia Alexander to her first meeting of directors. Patricia was formally co-opted as a director on 20th March 2006.

In her first message in Quarterly Return in the spring of 2006 Patricia gave a little background to herself:

"I'm delighted to have the opportunity to lead this organisation and consider it a privilege to be able to carry out such a personally fulfilling role.

"Before coming to Shared Interest I was Managing Director for Saint-

Gobain Quartz plc, and gained a great deal of experience working across international boundaries and cultures, which I'm sure will be valuable in this role. I'm a qualified accountant, a recent MBA graduate and am currently a member of the North East Industrial Development Board. I've also served locally as a member of the CBI Regional Council.

"These roles plus my work in the voluntary sector with St Cuthbert's Care and as Treasurer and Trustee of North Tyneside Carers Centre have given me a wide range of experience which I hope can benefit Shared Interest as we move forward at this very exciting time for our organisation."

At her second board meeting a month or two later, Patricia outlined her initial impressions. Her overall feeling was that the Society had come a long way in the last two years. Much had been achieved with limited resources. There was though she felt still a great deal of learning (from the Social Accounts and elsewhere) that needed to be built on. In particular Patricia felt a need to refresh the 'Delivering the Vision' focus.

In her first year in office, Patricia travelled to Europe and East Africa to meet some of Shared Interest's customers. She reported on her first trip to East Africa in Quarterly Return:

"I have just returned from my first trip to Kenya. I visited several of our partners including Mango True Mirage where our pilot producer training was carried out. They told me their business has benefited enormously from the training which is great news for the Foundation.

"I also had the opportunity to visit a community project supported by one of our handicraft customers, Undugu. They have opened schools in the slum areas of Nairobi to train 12-16 year olds in practical skills, so the social impact of our lending cascades far beyond our direct partners.

"Many of the African customers are facing real issues with financing their businesses and are heavily dependent on our support. I feel very privileged to have had the opportunity to visit these organisations where I was made

extremely welcome, and to see first hand the impact Shared Interest is having."

Patricia's visit to East Africa was timely as for the first time in the history of Shared Interest, producer lending had reached more than £1m. Quarterly Return reported that *"from a small beginning in Spring 1999 when just three producer groups borrowed less than £5,000 against buyer orders Shared Interest now has more than £1m lent to southern partners".*

With this increased lending to not only producers but buyers as well, the push for more investment was well under way and Philip Angier as Moderator of the Board called for action from members, in Quarterly Return in the spring of 2006.

Our social accounts for 2005 showed that 580,000 individuals in the Developing World benefited last year from the work of Shared Interest, a figure much greater than we had expected and evidence of the hugely beneficial impact of your investments. Last year £21.3m was advanced to finance fair trade orders, which means that every pound you invested was used at least once; and your investment does make a difference over and over again.

With the current level of support by our members, Shared Interest has achieved a great deal in its vision and mission; but the Society can do more with an even greater investment by all our members.

By lending more money to fair trade producers and buyers, we can have a greater impact on a greater number of individuals and communities. By lending more money directly to producers we can further help the sustainability of Developing World businesses. By lending more into commodities, such as coffee and bananas, we can

CHAPTER 11

increase the number of producers that benefit from your investments. By providing more low cost loans we can help more producers to grow their businesses and keep pace with the rapid growth of the fair trade movement. And, with our new overseas offices and local staff we are receiving increasing numbers of applications for finance from fair trade producer groups. We can only meet these requests for finance if we have additional investment which we can then lend to them.

To do this work, Shared Interest needs more share capital.

This need for more share capital was confirmed by the staff in the Africa and Latin America offices which were now up and running. They were receiving many applications and indeed sales were more than 40% ahead of budget at the time. However in reality margins on lending were reduced due to the weakness of the US dollar.

Hugo Villela in Quarterly Return Issue 60 described how he had been helping a number of groups to submit loan applications. One of these, a loan to Proagroin for $400,000, was agreed in the summer of 2006. The situation at Proagroin demonstrated the benefit of Shared Interest having a local representative. Shared Interest had approved a loan for the organisation the previous year but due to a change in management it had never been used. By meeting the new management face to face, Hugo was able to explain the details of the Shared Interest facility. As a result Proagroin applied for a larger loan, which it then went on to use.

In Africa, real benefits were being brought by the fact that Shared Interest shared an office with Traidcraft and COFTA (the Co-operation of Fair Trade Africa). They shared the services of an administrative assistant and producers when they visited were able to meet with all three organisations.

- 183 -

Their office building was also used by other fair trade organisations for training courses. *"The majority of producers are interested in loans for specific projects such as buying or renovating a building, drilling a borehole, buying a generator or fitting out a shop,"* said Rachel Ngondo, Shared Interest's Regional Development Executive for East Africa.

With increased demand from the overseas offices for more share capital there was also an internal assessment of how to maximise the return on capital already invested particularly as a fall in UK interest rates was anticipated by the year ahead. In particular understanding how much income was earned by lending to customers compared to for example, sitting on deposit with a European social bank, a policy which Shared Interest had pursued since inception.

In Issue 60 of Quarterly Return, published in the summer of 2006, the achievement of the £20m share capital was highlighted with enthusiasm. *"This is obviously a very significant milestone in the financial growth of the Society,"* said Company Secretary, Stuart Raistrick, *"and we have reached it just as we are expanding our activities to reach more producers across the developing world."*

Internally while the achievement of £20m share capital was exciting, it still felt disappointing that the Society had not been able to increase the number of members more quickly. Many people who were active in fair trade had still not heard of the Shared Interest Society. Later in the year an external agent was engaged to consider how to refresh the brand of Shared Interest with a view to increasing its appeal to a wider audience and the new brand was shared with members at the AGM in 2007.

From the start of her period as Managing Director, Patricia Alexander had stated a need to refresh the 'Delivering the Vision' focus of the organisation and so in 2007 she led the organisation through a thorough strategic review. Her priority was to determine how best to work with members, customers and partners to deliver an even greater reduction in poverty. In the plan that was presented to the Board in May 2007 there was an ambitious strategy to treble the money invested in Shared Interest over a five year period.

The work proposed was underpinned by a refreshed Vision, Mission and Values. Patricia Alexander said at the time that: *"These statements describe our ethos as a modern, dynamic fair trade business and our clear commitment to all the people who invest, borrow and work with us."*

Vision

We see a world where Shared Interest provides finance and business support to disadvantaged communities to enable them to trade their way out of poverty.

Mission

Our mission is to provide financial services and business support to make livelihoods and living standards better for disadvantaged communities in some of the world's poorest countries.

We work with people who share our commitment to fair and just trade. Together we take and share risk, because we value the difference that fair and sustainable trade makes.

We seek to satisfy the needs of producers as they work their way out of poverty and to meet the aspirations of our investors and donors to support them in achieving this aim.

Values

We will conduct our business in a manner which reflects the principles of love, justice and stewardship. We will:

- Work to recognised Fair Trade standards
- Respect the diversity of different cultures
- Value and engage our members and supporters
- Place partnership at the heart of what we do when working with others
- Work with our people and encourage their commitment, talents, and energy in an environment of mutual respect.

In a document sent out to all members, entitled 'We see the world as it could be', the Society outlined its five-year plan. Its goal was that: *"By 2012 Shared Interest will become the most respected provider of ethical finance and business support to disadvantaged producers globally."*

On the lending side, the priority continued to be supporting marginalised producers as they worked their way out of poverty. There were four main components to the plan:

- Treble the overall lending
- Lend significantly more to the growers and artisans than the businesses that buy, market and export their produce and goods by 2012
- Increase staffing in the countries and regions where Shared Interest's customers live and work
- Investigate partnerships with other social lenders and bodies representing marginalised communities.

It was felt overall that the 'Delivering the Vision' strategy had delivered good growth in lending but that it had not delivered the increase in investment needed going forward. As a consequence new goals were set for investment. It was recognised that fundamental to delivering these social gains was the

**The changing face of Quarterly Return
reflects the changing brand of Shared Interest**

strategy to treble the funds invested by UK supporters to £75m in 2012. In order to deliver the investment, Shared Interest committed to:

- Work more closely with current and new members to better understand their aspirations for the organisation
- Investigate whether there were other products that could be developed to meet members' hopes and expectations
- Change the way investment was marketed
- Develop partnerships with Fairtrade towns, universities, churches and schools
- Investigate partnerships with other Fair Trade and commercial businesses.

Internally of course, other debates were going on. Firstly, the present focus on only providing finance to fair trade organisations that were either members of IFAT or certified by FLO was discussed and the pros and cons of maintaining an exclusive fair trade focus was considered. This was raised because the business plan was strongly in favour of small, disadvantaged producers some of whom might be at risk of falling foul of changing IFAT entry standards. It was known that FLO and IFAT were both going through a process of change and it was hoped they would emerge in a stronger form. Whilst some internally felt a need to explore beyond the FLO / IFAT market should they fail to emerge stronger, overall the feeling was that if fair trade was growing why would the Society feel the need to reduce its focus on fair trade? It was clearly felt that as fair trade became *"mainstream"* there would be more demand for the Society's services among producers. This was alongside the concern about the costs of investigating and approving different certification schemes, of which there were thought to be in excess of 12 competing marks with similar standards to IFAT and FLO. It was emphasized that the Society had to rely on certification marks because of the prohibitive cost of doing its own fair trade verification. Staff keen to pursue a wider focus reflected that the change was similar to the broadening of the base of customers when the Society moved away from its exclusive IFAT focus. A more robust business would be built on a wider certification base.

On the investment side, there was a discussion about a much more member-focused approach in order to attract more investment. The possibility of attracting funds in Euros and US dollars was discussed although at the time there was a lot of caution expressed about raising capital outside the UK in currencies other than Sterling and doubts about any economic advantages were strongly expressed. To boost the member-focused approach, a new staff team, the Supporter Relations Team was established, headed up by Paul Sharpe as Supporter Relations Manager. The team included two

Supporter Relations Officers, who were tasked with raising the profile of Shared Interest and recruiting members in different parts of the UK. Also for the first time, a PR Manager was recruited to elevate the profile of Shared Interest in the press.

While strategy was being discussed in the office, more lending proposals were being approved and the range of customers expanded, as reported in Quarterly Return in the summer and autumn of 2007:

Wansananaa Self Help Group, Kenya

Another group of craft workers has started to use Shared Interest's financial services as a direct result of the Society's and Foundation's activities in East Africa.

Rachel Ngondo and Ben Lilley met with Eric Nyangate, the co-ordinator of Wanasanaa Self Help Group, at the African IFAT conference in May 2006. Later that year, Eric took part in training organized by Shared Interest Foundation at the Nairobi office. Now the group has started to use Shared Interest's export credit facility to make payments with orders to craft workers.

The group is a non-government organisation set up to help soapstone carvers in the town of Tabaka in western Kenya. 'Wanasanaa' means 'artists' in Swahili. The group was set up by 20 founder members and works with some 400 carvers.

Eric Nyangate is using the business skills he gained from the Foundation's training to increase productivity. In future the group is planning to build an office complex and design school.

Rungwe Smallholders Tea Growers Association, Tanzania

Rungwe Smallholders Tea Growers Association is using a loan from Shared Interest to buy a 4WD vehicle so it can deliver training and study visits to farmers in remote areas of the Rungwe district in south west Tanzania.

The association has 15,000 members, each farming less than half a hectare of land, spread over 108 villages. The association owns 25% of the Wakulima Tea Factory and has been supplying Cafédirect since 2002. Since then 100 new schools and 21 water projects have been built using income from the Fairtrade premium.

By 2008, discussions internally were looking at credit policy and prudential limits as the lending was increasing and starting to reach maximum limits of share capital. It was proposed that the 75% prudential limit could be breached occasionally as long as closely monitored. (The 75% limit at the time was designed to make it possible for the Society, without external borrowing, to service customer facilities and also offer members withdrawal of share capital on demand.) It was noted that there was also about £1m in the Society's reserves that could be available in addition to the share capital.

It was acknowledged that the prudential limit might in the future be calculated based on the total share capital and reserves less an amount for withdrawals. Or it might be more logical if the prudential limit was a ratio of share capital and reserves versus committed lending rather than the present ratio of drawn lending to share capital. What was clear was that as the 75% limit had been breached the limit needed to be reconsidered. Of course changes in the dollar/sterling exchange rate had an unpredictable effect on the amount of drawn and committed lending, which was always expressed in pounds sterling. At the end of 2008 it was agreed that the approved facilities should not be allowed to exceed 125% of share capital.

For the first time in the history of Shared Interest, discussions were starting to take place about what measures should be taken if lending was constrained due to share capital: should producer facilities be prioritised over buyers? Should large buyers be asked to reduce their facilities?

Overall the budget was being reviewed and towards the end of 2008 it was recalculated using more pessimistic assumptions (UK base rate 2% and exchange rate of $1.50 to £1). This clearly had an impact on the projected profit for the year which moved from £104,000 to -£15,000 with these changes.

By early 2009, it was confirmed in the discussion on the lending portfolio prudential limits that no new facilities had been approved since the board meeting in December 2008 but the prudential limit had varied from 124% to 138% of share capital due to changes in exchange rates. Facilities had been reduced in that period by £1.4m.

At the March 2009 meeting, there was a further discussion about bringing lending within the prudential limits. Charges for undrawn facilities were suggested as a mechanism for encouraging a reduction in the gap between drawn and committed lending. Seasonality in the Society's customer drawn balances had reduced. Drawn lending had peaked at 94% of share capital in 2008/9.

While it might free up some share capital, one key argument against reducing the facility limits of large buyer customers was that many producers depended on the orders from buyers. So for organisations like Ten Thousand Villages who are supported financially by the Mennonite Central Committee, taking the decision to reduce their facility limit might be acceptable, but the debate would then turn to what impact this would have on their producers accessing credit against their orders.

By this point in time, doubts were being expressed by the Board that share capital was growing or could grow as fast as was projected. US$ denominated loan stocks or share accounts were suggested as being ideas worth considering but it was emphasised that any commercial borrowing by the Society should be discussed by directors before proceeding. It was agreed that if lending proposals were satisfactory new lending to customers in East Africa up to a maximum of £100,000 could be approved.

One of the lending highlights of the year was detailed in Quarterly Return Issue 71 published in the spring of 2007 when co-operation of three of Shared Interest's customers resulted in Palestinian olive oil being brought to the UK:

Canaan Fair Trade in Jenin, Palestine, processes and bottles the oil on behalf of the Palestinian Fair Trade Producers Company. Zaytoun imports the oil and distributes it to specialist fair trade retailers and the "solidarity market". Equal Exchange wholesales to the delicatessen and natural foods market and to mainstream retailers. Palestinian Fairtrade olive oil is currently on sale in 300 branches of the Co-operative.

Shared Interest provides credit against the orders from Equal Exchange and Zaytoun which enables the Palestinian farmers to be paid in advance and in between harvests. Also in 2007 Shared Interest made a three year loan to help Canaan Fair Trade to build a new processing plant and storage facility.

Although managing the lending portfolio in the light of the current amount of share capital was important, it was emphasised by the Supporter Relations Team that there had been a noticeable acceleration in the number of new member accounts. Blogging and other methods were increasing the electronic presence of the Society. With a full Supporter Relations Team in post, it was pleasing to see that a number of initiatives were now being progressed so for example the number and diversity of ambassadors (formerly known as voluntary representatives) was increasing; school packs were on the point of being introduced and free press cover was increasing.

With the development of blogging and online social networking technologies, it is becoming increasingly easy to find and connect with like-minded individuals who may be interested in becoming members and/or spreading the word to their friends and acquaintances. While there are numerous social networking websites and technologies available, we have chosen to focus on developing a Shared Interest blog and utilising the following social networking sites: Flickr, Twitter, YouTube and Facebook.

As Shared Interest comes to the end of its financial year in 2009, it is celebrating the fact that lending to customers is at an all-time high and share capital has recently topped £26m. It knows that in order to continue to grow and develop Shared Interest will need to be innovative in its approach going forward, particularly looking for innovative ways to raise more capital as the market potential to lend more is clearly there. What better way to end than to celebrate a move made by Cafédirect that was reported in Quarterly Return in the summer of 2009:

Cafédirect reduces its borrowing needs and invests in Shared Interest
One of Shared Interest's most successful customers, the UK Fairtrade beverage pioneer Cafédirect, has made a double contribution to efforts to make more credit available to Fair Trade producers.

Richard Scanlon, Finance Director of Cafédirect plc explains:

"As the global recession bit hard in the UK late last year, Cafédirect was increasingly aware of the devastating effects of the banking crisis on producer partners. Growers were reporting that it was becoming extremely difficult to get pre-financing for the costs of growing their tea, coffee and cocoa. So when Shared Interest approached Cafédirect with the option to lower our credit facilities to enable increased lending to the growers, Cafédirect was quick to agree.

"One of the producer partners to benefit from this is Prodecoop, a cooperative based in Nicaragua that provides us with gourmet coffee for our Espresso, Cloud Forest and Medium Roast products. Cafédirect was delighted to hear that an additional $400,000 has been made available to them as a result of this joint initiative with Shared Interest."

MANGO TRUE MIRAGE

Mango True Mirage was established in 1998 and is based in the Machakos District of Kenya. They produce and supply Kenyan handicrafts that are both functional and decorative and made from various locally-available raw materials

CHAPTER 12
THE FUTURE

"If an organisation says it's not for change, then forget it."
Reverend Robert Waters, one of the first people to invest in Shared Interest

———◆———

A fter this gallop through the history of Shared Interest what better way to finish than to turn our thoughts to the future of the organisation. With a significant amount achieved during the last twenty years, how will the organisation develop over the next twenty years?

As we don't have a crystal ball, the last word will be left with those who have contributed to the story so far:

"Broadly speaking the organisation is growing quite well. It is important to bear in mind that it takes several decades to build strong financial institutions, if not centuries. It is inevitable that there will be hiccups over the years. I do hope it sticks to its knitting – lending to fair trade producers.

"Overall I am very happy with how the business has evolved. The current excess demand for Shared Interest's lending products is good. Lending rates will have to increase and it will have to become more profitable. Similarly saving rates will have to increase. I don't really see investment rising much

without the saving rates increasing. It is quite possible that the share capital will stay roughly as it is for a few years but will then increase once the organisation becomes profitable.

My major concern is that after a long period of successful work on the Society's business we now need to do more work again on the Society itself – i.e. on democratic engagement with members. Communication with members has become steadily more 'corporate' and I cannot recall the last time members were asked to make a meaningful decision, or even when the Board shared a major dilemma. The recent final decoupling from Oikocredit was a lost opportunity: members as a whole should have been more involved, but the matter was treated as a narrowly commercial decision for Management alone. Part of the distinctive attraction of Shared Interest was the sense of ownership, of gaining some understanding and control over the black box of finance: being a good cause is, I'm afraid, not enough."

Mark Hayes, Principal Founder and first Managing Director

"In the next 20 years I'd like the public to know as much about SI as they do about the fair trade movement. We need to become better known, increase our membership and diversify our target audience. I'd like to see the process to open an account made more accessible, by enabling people to invest £10 in a month until they have the minimum of £100 to open an account."

Tracy Mitchell, Ambassador

"I would like to see Shared Interest take investment from around the world. Shared Interest clones in different currencies, it might be dollars and euros or more widespread than that.

"It should continue to be anchored at the heart of the Fair Trade movement both conceptually but also through the networks of IFAT and FLO.

"I would like to see it have a higher profile in the UK. From an informed

member's perspective the profile hasn't changed over the years.

"I would also like to see it offer a variety of lending products. A real armoury of offerings, which would enable it to manage the risk more effectively."

Stephanie Sturrock, Managing Director, Shared Interest 1998 - 2005

"To be better known... that fair trade survives and is not knocked to the side by something else. I believe fair trade will survive the recession and continue to help producers trade their way out of poverty.

"I would like to see us with many, many multiples of £25m to lend, and having at least ten times as many members; in 20 years' time, we ought to have at least 100,000 members. Hundreds of thousands of people buy fair trade, why shouldn't they support it in other ways too? Imagine what it would mean to fair trade producers if Shared Interest's membership were to grow to 100,000 and each member invested £10 a month!

"The world of finance will have changed in 20 years' time in ways that I cannot begin to envisage but, I still think that what Shared Interest does will be important and there will continue to be contributions to the Shared Interest effort."

Carol Wills, Board member

"Shared Interest is a pioneering organisation that continues to do amazing work. It is very admiral. It is a very special model that no one else does.

"The labelling part of Fairtrade has been copied by many (Rainforest Alliance etc), however Shared Interest has not and that is because it is unique. It concentrates on what it does best helping disadvantaged producers access fair finance and all the impacts that this makes on the producers, their families and the communities in which they work.

"What I would like to see Shared Interest do is to become less UK centric,

why not have an office in Brussels and open up what you do to the whole of Europe. This would help with investment and raise your profile.

"I would also like to see the Foundation provide small loans to assist producers to get on the fair trade ladder.

"I think it is brilliant that you have internationalised in terms of regional offices which assist your producers, why not internationalise the other part of your business into Europe and America.

"I would like Shared Interest to keep a balance between the number of producers it supports and buyers. As many buyers are really struggling (especially in light of the current economic climate), as without strong buyers there will be no market for those producers to sell to and without a market they will have no business, no livelihood and there will be no fair trade."
Hilary Thorndike, former IFAT Membership Officer

"It feels like there is a lot to do as Shared Interest moves into its 21st year – quite appropriate really! I think the Society and Foundation are at a very interesting point with wider lending and greater share capital than ever but a world where recent economic norms have been turned upside-down and fair trade itself is at a fascinating cross-roads. For me, it's great to be joining Shared Interest at this moment. I know I'm privileged to be coming into a great team, which is being further strengthened as others join now too. I would just ask our supporters to maintain and where possible increase their efforts to help us in the fight against poverty. Here's to the next 20 years!"
Tim Morgan, Board member

"Conditions are ripe for a dramatic transformation of financial services. How will Shared Interest and the international development movement respond? Will they show the same vision and leadership that has taken Fairtrade from pretty disgusting coffee for the deeply committed 20 years ago to a whole range

of products that taste great, are cool to buy and mainstream supermarkets can't ignore? Shared Interest has had a solid first 20 years – but today it is still the equivalent of that 1990 Fairtrade coffee. It is not a financial services version of Cafédirect.

"After the financial crisis, there is a real opportunity for new thinking about savings and investment – for financial products that make money and make a difference. Many people, particularly younger people, should be saving for retirement – but they aren't. They can afford to take a certain level of risk because time is on their side – but too often they are not inspired by the investment opportunities available today. Can international development champions help them invest their money in developing countries in ways that make financial sense and deliver added social returns. Leading NGOs like Oxfam and WWF are exploring how to transform the City, but a lesson from Fairtrade is to compete with current providers as well. To help, there is knowledge about disruptive innovation from other fields, and the power of the internet to tap into skills, experience and networks across the globe.

"Shared Interest now needs to make a significant choice. It can continue in its niche, helping the minority who are willing to do good while sacrificing financial returns. Or it can transform itself into a new modern mould-breaking international development investment manager, ready to compete with anything that mainstream financial services can offer. Or continue as now while catalysing change elsewhere. Which will it chose?"
Penny Shepherd, UKSIF

"People around the world are living with many of the consequences of the financial crisis and associated economic downturn. Shared Interest provides a living demonstration of an alternative approach to financial services: based on strong values yet delivering practical action through money, to use the market for people rather than the other way around. I hope that we can see

this particular approach flourish successfully, and inspire others to find new ways to serve the needs especially of poor people."
David Nussbaum, Board member

"In the future I would like to see the profile of Shared Interest increase as there is definitely a demand to do so. Specifically, I'd like more people to become aware of the business and financial aspects surrounding the fair trade movement and would like Shared Interest to target larger corporate investment. I recently did a talk at the Ethical Businesses Club in Oxford which was well received, but given the hardships which small businesses are facing I think the way forward for investment are larger organisations."
Mike McKinley, Ambassador

"Shared Interest can be a conduit to help consumers support different types of Fair Trade at different levels of risk. I have been investing with Shared Interest for 20 years and would like Shared Interest to be bolder in investing in pioneering start-ups – people like me, even at 20, don't care so much about getting their money.

"Shared Interest needs more support from the general public to scale up its support to social businesses, especially outside the Fair Trade food area – today, this is where mainstreaming needs to go. Fairtrade clothing and crafts is the obvious next area for support. Go, Shared Interest!"
Safia Minney, CEO People Tree

"It would be nice to see Shared Interest establish themselves in the US or other countries and take advantage of the capital available."
Bob Chase, CEO SERRV

"Passionate people have literally changed the world of trade and the lives

of millions. Shared Interest has a proud heritage as part of the fair trade movement. Its future rests in adapting to changing times, embracing its values and making sure we continue to support those endeavouring to trade sustainably. As Chair Elect, I feel a particular responsibility that all the tremendous work of the last twenty years and the commitment of our members is cherished and built on. With pride and passion we continue our important work."
Kate Priestley, Chair Elect

"SI needs to use new technology to link members directly with producers as well as finding a way to include and engage corporate members. SI is good at credit risk assessment – by sharing this with members, members then have the option to invest directly (online) with individual projects so you don't have the problem of a £20,000 limit.

"It's also great to have people on the ground close to the producers who speak the same language and have a real understanding of the situation in country. These networks need to continue to be developed."
Stuart Raistrick, former Board and staff member

"The vision for the future of SI relates really to achieving the goals that have already been set by management, especially the £75m goal. Also to see the spread of Regional Offices to cover further parts of the world, including India and Asia. On a personal level, my own vision is my being surrounded by friends, colleagues etc who are supportive of and investors in Shared Interest."
Ralph Nicholas Eales, Ambassador

"My vision for Shared interest will be the same as yours, I want it to continue to grow, increase loan and share capital and help many more producers

throughout the Developing World. The concept that Mark established was correct from the word go, so it's just about increasing share and loan capital to help more and more people."
Chris Ruck, first Moderator of the Board

"For Shared Interest to be more widely known and mainstream. There are issues for the regulatory environment – if something was to go wrong in Shared Interest (losing members' money). Trying to raise our profile but not with regulators."
Jenny Hamilton, former Council member (and Moderator of the Council)

"I would like to see steady growth in the future. I think it would be interesting to see if corporate investment might become significant particularly if the current £20,000 limit is raised."
Geoff Moore, former Moderator of the Board

"I want the world to be fairer with everyone able to access banking in their own country. I want everyone to live reasonably well, receive a decent wage, acceptable standards of education and for Shared Interest to become redundant or convert into an International Bank after it has been overtaken by a fairer world!"
Joan Stableford, Ambassador

"I would like to think that SI will be doing much of what it is doing today. It wouldn't be surprising to see SI become a bank. I think this would be a good thing for the banking world and something different.

"Today people see banks as organisations that are there purely to make money and people don't have much faith in them. If a new type of bank came

on the scene it would be a good thing and SI could play this role.

"FT awareness in the UK is growing – much more than in the US. There are of course fears that FT will be diluted by the involvement of organisations such as Cadbury etc so it is important to keep people motivated and educated about what FT is and what a positive difference it can make to the lives of people in developing countries."
Colin Crawford, former Operations Director

"As for the future, my experience of around 40 years around the cooperative movement is that small cooperatives are more successful than large ones in holding to their objectives. E.F.Schumacher's 'Small is Beautiful' remains a strong influence. So Shared Interest might consider:
1. Splitting into two linked but independent cooperative societies (one for 'east' and one for 'west'?). Daily Bread Co-operative, which started trading in 1980 in Northampton, made a split of this kind in 1992 by supporting a new independent cooperative in Cambridge, rather than 'opening a branch' which would have become a subsidiary.
2. Changing from a 'consumer cooperative', owned and formally controlled by its 8,000 investing members, to a 'worker cooperative', owned by its staff, with restrictions about the disposal of the business and leaving certain residuary powers in the hands of the investors, represented by the Council. Here again, there are precedents within the cooperative movement for this type of structure.

"I realise these are radical ideas which will frighten some and which would need long debate before action, but Shared Interest would never have happened without some out-of-the-box thinking and determination by the founders."
Roger Sawtell, Founder Member

"It would be wonderful if Shared Interest were 10 times bigger and have 10 times the impact in the Third World. More funds – more impact. Shared Interest has to pay its way to be commercially viable. Shared Interest's charges to its customers represent good value compared with what they could get elsewhere."

Richard Butchart, former Moderator of the Council

"I would like to see Shared Interest achieve your/their ambitious investment goals. I think there needs to be a step change in order to do this.

"I would like to see the £20,000 limit cracked, so that people who would like to invest more are able to do so. I would also like to see the £100 limit lowered so that it enables everyone who would like to invest to invest without limitations.

"I would like to see the Foundation continue to grow.

"I would like Shared Interest to find a way to convey our message and get it out there, to advertise and bring in more money which will enable us to lend more out – it's that simple.

"To go from £25m to £100m."

Michael Walton, former Board member

"View of 20 years' time? Share capital in excess of £250m and providing more advice to fair trade with an expanded range of products and services especially for small producers. Having good financial reports is vital to a business, it is like oxygen is to the human body.

"If I was to speak to your AGM I would say to our members that the original idea was really good and has been implemented very well however over time we have become cautious and risk adverse. I would challenge you to launch something significant and additional for the next 20 years."

Paul Myers, President of the World Fair Trade Organization (WFTO)

"Shared Interest has demonstrated the resilience and sustainability of its business model. We must avoid complacency, but definitely the challenge is to expand significantly the scale of our activities. We need to rise to that challenge because fair trade worldwide is growing – and especially so in the UK. If fair trade is a £1 billion per year business, it will need £250m to £350m of working capital finance. That's 10 times bigger than Shared Interest at present.

"Shared Interest also needs to make its model of social investment better known. The melt-down of the banking system in 2008/2009 has led investors to re-evaluate their priorities. Maybe socially sustainable lending is more interesting than a hedge fund – especially when we the taxpayer find that we are forced to become the lender of last resort to misguided financiers. In this context we face competition from new web-based models which link individual investors direct with borrowers.

"Our embryonic network of Regional Offices offer the opportunity both to understand better the needs of growers and producers around the world and to increase our social impact by targeting our lending where it is most needed. There is tremendous power – both economic and social – in the willingness of investors in one hemisphere of the world to share access to finance and to share risk with farmers and producers in the other.

"Shared Interest Foundation is still an infant in the Shared Interest family. It has already proved its worth. Before new customers can borrow with confidence, or Shared Interest can lend, skills need to be developed, and organisational capacity strengthened. The whole Shared Interest story is about steps towards greater self-reliance for our customers. The Foundation can do much useful work to make those first steps surer."
Philip Angier, Chairman of the Board

"I've become more acutely aware of a very simple but powerful fact – that the money we members of the Society invest to make a positive difference in people's lives across the world is used, not just once, but over and over again.

"I definitely feel new possibilities have opened up through the current financial crisis. I might have given a different answer to this question 18 months ago! The pitch has changed. Shared Interest has real opportunities to take advantage of. Now it would seem there may even be capacity within Third World countries – all sorts of interesting ideas are coming out of the business community within India at the moment for example."
Richard Adams, Founder Member

"In the future I would like to see organisations in other countries affiliated to Shared Interest, so that many more people have the opportunity to invest and our unique financial service can reach many more producers."
Margaret Newens, Ambassador

"£75m – well I have to say that even when we came up with that figure we felt it was pretty ambitious – but you have to have goals that stretch you. There is a part of me that would aim for more members than more money. By having more members we have more people who can spread the word and who we can encourage to give more money. But I don't think there are any quick wins; we need to be strategic (about boosting income and membership).

"I think Board members could do more, and that the Board and Council could work harder at bringing in members, we should all be ambassadors. I think the idea of being an ambassador is a very good one. We need them, but we could make more of the role and get the ambassadors doing more.

"I think social media and online communications is a fabulous opportunity for Shared Interest. We could really push it more, especially if we're looking to target younger members. We need to have a truly integrated approach to all *our communications. One of the lovely things is that we've got all those great stories about our work overseas. Through social media we could be blogging and tweeting these around the world. Becoming more active online means that we may also get to online banking too which could make accessing things easier for our members."*

Gill Dandy, Board member

"Shared Interest has proved itself to be invaluable to the artisans and farmers who access our finance; it is vital that our capacity to lend grows with their determination to earn a fair living.

"The individuals I meet during my overseas trips are so full of energy and inspiration. I am writing this on my first day back from a trip to our Kenya office. It is impossible not to feel inspired, if not a little overwhelmed by the people and places I visit when travelling overseas. The nature of fair trade is that businesses not only work hard to ensure they thrive but that they also help others work their way out of the poverty they were born into.

"Without our loyal members, we could not continue to support those who may have no other access to finance – at least not at an affordable rate.

"I hope and believe we can achieve £100m share capital in the not so distant future with additional overseas offices to reach those people who really need our services either through the Society or our charitable arm, the Foundation.

"As we launch this commemorative book in our twentieth year, it provides a perfect opportunity for reflection. Without doubt, everyone who is, or has been, connected with Shared Interest's work should be very proud of the success so far. However, this is no time to rest on our laurels because to meet the huge demand for fair finance, there is so much more still to be done."

Patricia Alexander, Managing Director

APPENDIX

SHARED INTEREST STAFF AS AT 1ST MARCH 2010

Rachel Abel
Patricia Alexander
Geoff Atkinson
David Belk
Kirsteen Bonar
Jane Burns
Tina Chapman
Ann Colquhoun
Malcolm Curtis
Christina Dodds
Shirley Fletcher
Adam Gaines
Cherianne Hudson
Andrew Jones
Raquel Lee Vargas
Louise McLaren
Amy Milne
Tim Morgan
Rachel Ngondo
Jane Njora
Sally Reith
Andrew Ridley
Paul Sablich
Paul Sharpe
Ruth Taylor
Joanne Tong
Stacey Toth
Hugo Villela
Andrea Wilkinson
Steven Willis
Ashleigh Wilson
Elisabeth Wilson
Margaret Woodhouse

COUNCIL

Richard Butchart
(to March 10th)
Kate Guggenheim
Ann Hillier
Trevor Jones
Stephen Sanders
Denis Stewart
(to March 10th)
John Crowch
(to March 10th)
Claire Wigg
Mary Willcox
(Moderator)
(to March 10th)
Jo Bird
(from March 10th)
Margaret Newens
(from March 10th)

BOARD
NON EXECUTIVE

Philip Angier
Stacey Toth
(Chair)
Kate Priestley
(Chair Elect)
Gill Dandy
Peter Freeman
Ruth McIntosh
David Nussbaum
Carol Wills

EXECUTIVE

Patricia Alexander
(Managing Director)
Tim Morgan
(Finance Director)

PRODUCERS

Alternative Trade
Network of Nigeria
Apicoop Valdivia
Cooperativa Campesina
Apicola
Aprainores – Asociación
de Productores
Agroindustriales
Orgánicos de El
Aprocassi
Asasapne
Asociacion Chajulense
Va'l Vaq Quyol
Bega Kwa Bega
Korogocho Projects

CAC Bagua Grande Ltda

CAC Oro Verde

Cacvra – Coop Agraria

Cafetelera Valle Rio Apurimac Ltd

Café Peru SAC

Canaan Fair Trade Company

Candela Peru

Cecocafen RL

Cenfrocafe

Cocla – Central de Cooperativas Agrarias Cafeteleras

Cepicafe

Ciapec

Cocagi Cooperative

Coinacapa – Cooperativa Integral Agroextractivista

Comparte

Coocafe

Coopecañera – Cooperativa Cancra

Craft Aid (Mauritius) Co Ltd

Dezign Incorporated (PVT) Ltd

Dukunde Kawa Cooperative (Musasa)

Eco Caraigres Agricola SA

Eloc Farms Limited

Fair Packers (Pty) Ltd

Fruits of the Nile (U) Ltd

Fundación Solidaridad Talleres Artesanales

Gebana Afrique

Gebana Brasil

Grupo Agricola Prieto

Handicrafts Marketing Company (Mikono)

Holyland Handicrafts

Intercrafts Peru SAC

Java Ixora

Kenya Gatsby Trust

La Alianza

Mabale Growers Tea Factory Ltd

Mace Foods

Mpanga Growers Tea Factory Ltd

Much In Little Inc

Namayiana Oloshoibor Maasai Women's Group

NAWOU

Nyabigena Soapstone Carvers Organisation

Proagroin

Prodecoop RL

RSTGA

Salay Handmade Paper Industries Inc

Salom Enterprises Ltd

Smolart Self Help Group

South Organic

Temak

Trinity Jewellery Crafts

UCA San Juan de Rio Coco

UCPCO – Union de Cooperativas Productoras de Café Orgánico

Ucraprobex de RL de CV

Undugu Society of Kenya

VREL – Volta River Estates Ltd

Xochipilli ACy Xochiquetzal SAdeCV

BUYERS

Agrofair Europe BV

Au–délà des Frontières

Cafédirect plc

CTM Altromercato Soc Coop ARL

DWP

El Puente GmbH

Epona Limited

Equal Exchange Inc

Equal Exchange Trading Ltd

Ethicalsuperstore.com Limited

EZA

Fairwind Trading Company Limited

Fullwell Mill Limited

Gebana BV

GoGo Quinoa

La Siembra Cooperative Inc

Laarsen Associates Inc

Liberation Foods CIC

Liberomondo

Magasins du Monde Oxfam

One World Shop

Oxfam Australia Trading Pty Ltd

Oxfam Quebec Inc

People Tree

Roba Dell'Altro Mondo
SERRV International Inc
Sustainable Harvest
Coffee Importers (USA)
Ten Thousand Villages
– Canada

Ten Thousand Villages
– US
The House of Fair Trade
Traidcraft plc
Tropical Forest Products
Ltd

Vericott Ltd t/a
Gossypium
Wayfairer Ltd
World of Good Inc
Zaytoun CIC

SHARED INTEREST TIMELINE

1986 Mark Hayes, Investment Manager at 3i, contacted Richard Adams, Managing Director Traidcraft with a proposal for a Development Bank

1987 Mark Hayes secondment to Traidcraft to explore potential for an alternative investment entity

1989 Mark Hayes employed by Traidcraft and developed a business plan for an alternative investment organisation, named at the time as TraidShare

1990 Shared Interest founded and registered as an Industrial and Provident Society, separate to Traidcraft with Mark Hayes as its first Managing Director
At the end of its first five months of trading, £350,000 invested in Shared Interest allowed the Ecumenical Development Cooperative Society to support 13 new projects in the Developing World
Board and Council established

1991 First Shared Interest Representatives appointed
First direct investments made to Bridgehead, trading subsidiary of OXFAM Canada, Traidcraft plc, Verdin, Huddersfield based importer of Peruvian craft products

1992 £1m share capital achieved in November
Largest direct investment to date, £85,000 to Traidcraft plc

1993 New premises: 31 Mosley Street, Newcastle upon Tyne

Decision taken to not speculate on Black Wednesday, September 1993 which could have earned the Society as much as £350,000 but it was felt that members did not invest their money to speculate and destabilise their own economy

1994   £5m share capital achieved

1995   AGM decision taken by members to be independent from EDCS and a new way of supporting EDCS through a Bond issue was promoted

1996   £10m share capital achieved

Staff team expanded – Operations Director and Producer Liaison Officer recruited

1997   Mark Hayes announced his intention to retire at 1999 AGM

Debate with the Bank of England over whether Shared Interest by issuing Loan Stock was operating an unauthorised deposit-taking (bank) business

The Council introduced a system of random nomination of four of its nine members from the membership in 1997

Members: 7,273 • Share Capital: £12.5m • Staff numbers: FT 5, PT 2

1998   New offices in Collingwood Street, Newcastle upon Tyne opened by Clare Short, Secretary of State for International Development

Shared Interest attempted to rescue Bridgehead, trading subsidiary of OXFAM Canada in order to help those producers that stood to lose what Bridgehead owed them. The rescue attempt ended two years later in failure and accounted for the largest bad debt Shared Interest has suffered to date

Stephanie Sturrock appointed as the new Managing Director

Shared Interest IFAT Clearing House established

Members: 8,315 • Share Capital: £14.9m • Staff numbers: FT 8, PT 2

1999   Within a year of establishing the Clearing House, nine producers had drawn on their account and borrowed £57,000

Members: 8,616 • Share Capital: £15.9m • Staff numbers: FT 10, PT 1

2000   Emerging Producer Scheme and Term Loans for producers were added to the range of financial products offered through the Clearing House

Members: 8,498 • Share Capital: £16.3m • Staff numbers: FT 11, PT 3

2001 Mark Hayes stepped down from the Board of Shared Interest

Board set a revised minimum interest rate of 0% (previously 1% reflecting the drop of the UK base rate to below 4%). From December interest rate to members was 0%.

Hilary Thorndike appointed into a new post, IFAT Membership Officer, sponsored by Shared Interest with the intention of expanding the membership base of IFAT

Membership survey

Members: 8,459 • Share Capital: £17.2 • Staff numbers: FT 11, PT 3

2002 Pilot study into lending more to coffee producers prepared which led to a collaboration with the World Bank's International Task Force

Shared Interest extended its Clearing House products to FLO certified Fairtrade producers

Members: 8,352 • Share Capital: £17.8m • Staff numbers: FT 13, PT 3

2003 50th edition of Quarterly Return published

Delivering the Vision project initiated – early views on establishing an international presence

Shared Interest jointly hosted with Traidcraft IFAT's 7th biennial conference at the University of Newcastle upon Tyne. More than 250 people from 50+ countries attended

Mission statement for the organisation revised

Shared Interest set up its charity arm, Shared Interest Foundation

Members: 8,194 • Share Capital: £17.7m • Staff numbers: FT 15, PT 3

2004 Coffee scorecard created which allowed Shared Interest to increase its lending to coffee producers

First experience of using consultants in the field to represent Shared Interest

Members: 8,344 • Share Capital: £18.4m • Staff numbers: FT 18, PT 1

2005 Business cases to set up a Regional Presence in Kenya and Costa Rica approved by the Board

First set of social accounts prepared for Shared Interest

Stephanie Sturrock resigned as Managing Director
Members: 8,354 • Share Capital: £19.2m • Staff numbers: FT 18, PT 3

2006 Patricia Alexander appointed as new Managing Director of Shared Interest
Staff recruited in Kenya and Costa Rica
First producer training project undertaken by Shared Interest Foundation
Producer lending more than £1m
£20m share capital achieved
Members: 8,402 • Share Capital: £20.5m •Staff numbers: FT 20, PT 2

2007 Strategic review defined by a refreshed Vision, Mission and Values statement
Members: 8,447 • Share Capital: £21.7m • Staff numbers: FT 22, PT 2

2008 Foundation awarded a large grant by the Big Lottery Fund to train fair trade producers in Rwanda
Possibility lending might be constrained by available share capital
Awarded the Queen's Award for Enterprise
Members: 8,668 • Share Capital: £26.1m • Staff numbers: FT 24, PT 3

2009 Staff recruited in Peru
By 2009 Foundation had trained 167 producer groups and over 250 people in seven countries
Share capital more than £26m
Members: 8,743 • Share Capital: £26.1m • Staff numbers: FT 25, PT 3